Becoming Mr. Right

A Young Man's Guide to God-Honoring Relationships

By Michael J. Daniels

Becoming Mr. Right
A Young Man's Guide to God-Honoring Relationships

ISBN 978-1-936141-38-8

Printed in the United States of America

Focus Publishing
PO Box 665
Bemidji, Minnesota 56619

ENDORSEMENTS

"A lot of people think the secret to a great marriage is finding the right person. Michael Daniels knows that it's about something even more important: *becoming* the right person."

Jim Daly, President
Focus on the Family

"This small book is well-written, biblical and very practical. It will be useful for young men today. I am not aware of any other book like it. Especially valuable are the application questions at the end of each chapter."

Dr. Wayne Mack, Biblical Counselor
Author of *Strengthening Your Marriage*

"Christian bookstore shelves are loaded with books on relationships. Sadly, few source their ideas and advice in Scripture. This unfortunate dearth makes Michael Daniels's *Becoming Mr. Right* stand out for those seeking to honor God and His Word in their relationships. Don't be fooled by the title! This book is for men and women. It highlights the man to become and the man to find. I trust it will find a wide reading from serious believers who are serious about relationships."

Dr. Rick Holland, Senior Pastor
Mission Road Bible Church
Kansas City, KS

"*Becoming Mr. Right* is a thoughtful, heartfelt, and thoroughly biblical treatment of a topic essential to the next generation of young men—the burden of carrying forward a strong and vibrant witness for Christ through godly families. Earnest young Christian men will want to read, learn, and practice these principles."

H. L. Johnson, Pastor
Twin Cities Bible Church
Maplewood, Minnesota

Dedication

This book is dedicated to my future son,
if God so blesses me with the privilege of fatherhood.

"Watch over your heart with all diligence,
for from it flow the springs of life."
- Proverbs 4:23 (NASB)

Acknowledgments

"Do not withhold good from those to whom it is due when it is in your power to do it."
- Proverbs 3:27

Many people have left a significant impact on my life, and contributed to the development of this book. Without them, the publishing of this work would never have been possible.

First of all, I would like to thank my dear wife, Mandy. She has been a faithful companion, and has taught me much about purity. She was the one who gave me the idea to write this book in the first place. She spent many hours tirelessly writing proposals, contributing to content, and making revisions. I can relate with Proverbs 31:28-29 which says, " ... her husband ... praises her, saying: 'Many daughters have done nobly, but you excel them all.'" I am indebted to all of her hard work and patience through many late nights.

I am grateful for my parents, Kevin and Kristie, who provided immeasurable amounts of love, loyalty, and guidance throughout my youth. I wouldn't be where I am today without their support.

I have been blessed with in-laws who've shaped much of my outlook on life in my early adult years. My mother-in-law, Judy, has been a model of genuine sensitivity and care for others. Through his example, my father-in-law, Walt, has instilled in me a passion to value God's words over the counsel of man.

The love, loyalty, and humor of my dear brothers, Tyler and Matthew, have brought much joy and comfort to my life. I can't imagine life without either of them. Their contribution to the content of this book has proved to be invaluable.

My brother in Christ, Andy Johnson, has been my faithful friend for longer than I can remember. His steadfast encouragement throughout my difficult high school and college years has made a lasting impact on my life.

My pastor, Lloyd Johnson, has faithfully counseled me throughout my entire life. He was instrumental in helping me navigate through difficult issues (including relationships) in my younger years. His mentorship continues to leave a significant impact on my life. I am thankful for the many hours he spent assessing my book's content.

My church elder, Jim Seifert, played a role in bringing me to the faith through his youth ministry. Through his example, he has taught me much about biblical manhood. Also, his pre-marital advice set a solid foundation for my marriage. I am thankful for his eagerness to review this book even in the midst of a very busy schedule.

In addition to those previously mentioned, I want to express gratitude to all the people who took time to review and contribute to this book's content: Steven Amis, Michael Delahunt, Luke Findell, Jeff Johnson, Tony Johnson, Tim Meehan, Caleb Milbrath, Isaac Milbrath, Patrick Monthe, Ben Peralez, Luke Rable, Cassie Schultze, and Bruce White. The enriching input of these individuals has influenced much of this book's content, and will, Lord willing, impact the hearts of many.

I am very thankful for the young men that God has blessed me with the privilege of mentoring. Their friendships provided me with the inspiration to write this book.

I would like to express appreciation to Jan Haley, President of Focus Publishing, who has taken this first-time author's manuscript, and shaped it to become a more effective tool for God's glory.

I also wanted to give credit to Pastor Rick Holland whose audio sermons revolutionized my perspective on romantic relationships.

Most importantly, I give all credit and glory to my Lord and Savior Jesus Christ. He was the One Who instilled a desire in my heart to write this book, and provided the means to complete it. I pray that this book will fulfill exactly what His will is, whatever that may look like.

Table of Contents

Acknowledgments vii

Introduction xiii

Chapter 1: Your Most Important Relationship 1

Chapter 2: The Man to Become 9

Chapter 3: Contentment 19

Chapter 4: Establishing Purity 27

Chapter 5: Practical Preparations 37

Chapter 6: Helping Your Fellow Sisters 45

Chapter 7: Rethinking "Love" 53

Chapter 8: Marriage-Mindedness 61

Chapter 9: The Woman to Find 67

Chapter 10: Initiating a Relationship 77

Chapter 11: Conduct in a Relationship 89

Chapter 12: Your Future Role 99

Chapter 13: Marriage is Not the End Goal 109

Conclusion 117

Appendices 121

- Appendix A: Preparing to Provide 123
- Appendix B: Singleness 127
- Appendix C: Breaking Up 131

Introduction

*"His divine power has granted to us all things
that pertain to life and godliness ... "*
- 2 Peter 1:3

How do I find "The One"? Throughout history, men of all backgrounds have sought answers in the search for a soulmate. Men often desire a woman who is charming, beautiful, and smart. But what if this journey has less to do with finding a perfect woman, and more to do with becoming the right man?

Becoming "Mr. Right"

God holds you accountable for your own character, and not for someone else's actions. Because this is true, it is important to place a greater emphasis on becoming the right person before God over finding your "perfect match." Think about it, if every man is caught up with looking for the right woman, but is not growing spiritually, then how will a girl ever find "Mr. Right"? The same is true about your own search. If women you consider do not grow in character, how will you ever find "Ms. Right"? It is much more important to focus on refining your own character, rather than allowing your life to become dominated with a search for a spouse.

What You Will Get Out of This Book

Whether you are single or in a relationship, this book is equally applicable to you. Here, you will learn how to apply Scripture to your life as you prepare to be worthy of the woman who you may someday marry. Rather than a "step-by-step" book on relationships, we will focus on developing character traits that are essential to relationships and marriage. Some of these key qualities include salvation, contentment, humility, purity, and a teachable spirit.

This book will also provide practical preparations in the areas of timing, education, and finance. In addition, you will discover the importance of marriage-mindedness and honorable conduct in a relationship. Finally, we will take a brief look at your future role as a husband, and how to maintain a balanced perspective toward the purpose of marriage.

If you are single, you will be encouraged to evaluate your own character before pursuing a woman. In addition, you will learn about key character qualities to look for in a woman. If you are already in a relationship, you will be challenged to consider areas for improvement in personal character, marriage-mindedness, and Christ-centeredness.

What You Do Now Will Impact Your Future

Every choice you make has consequences. Good decisions have good results. Bad decisions have bad results. Throughout your life, you will face decisions regarding friendships, careers, finances, entertainment, purity, and much more. These decisions will not only impact your life, but also the lives of your future wife and children. In order to begin setting a foundation for your future marriage, you must learn how to make wise choices now. If you haven't been serious about preparing for marriage in the past, let this book be your starting point.

The Bible's Relevancy to Relationships

I have heard many young people say, "Since the Bible doesn't have much to say about relationships, I can do whatever I want!" Some have even claimed that the Bible is outdated and not applicable to today's culture. On the contrary, Scripture has much to offer when it comes to the topic of relationships. 2 Peter 1:3 says, "His divine power has granted to us all things that pertain to life and godliness ..." Since God's Spirit and Word provide us with all we need regarding how we should conduct our lives, we can be assured that the Bible is absolutely relevant to relationships.

Our World Needs Godly Leaders

Society suffers in the absence of godly husbands and fathers. It is crucial for young men everywhere to step up and lead their families, communities, and countries in ways that honor God. But, in order to do this, we need to start with personal character. Proverbs 4:23 says, "Watch over your heart with all diligence, for from it flow the springs of life" (*NASB*). Since all of life's issues stem from the intent of peoples' hearts, you must be serious about assessing your spiritual condition. It is critical for every Christian to guard their heart against Satan's corrupting influences, and to equip themselves with the armor of God (*Ephesians 6:10-18*). The next generation of men must step up, and be lights for Christ in an ever-dimming world.

Beginning Your Own Journey

With all of this in mind, are you ready to explore what it takes to become "Mr. Right?" Let's jump in, and see what Scripture has to offer regarding the topic of relationships.

CHAPTER 1

Your Most Important Relationship

"But seek first the kingdom of God and His righteousness, and all these things will be added to you."
- Matthew 6:33

I'm sure you must be eager to dive into topics such as "who to marry" and "how to approach relationships." But before doing that, it's critical to evaluate the quality of *your most important relationship*. Specifically, what is the status of your relationship with God? Is your walk with Christ deep and meaningful? Or is He simply an afterthought? Without His guidance, you have no assurance that your efforts will be blessed. It is vital to ensure that you are right with God *first* before you begin or continue pursuing a young lady.

Implications of a Christ-less Relationship

Jesus said, "... apart from me you can do nothing" (*John 15:5*). Without Christ, you have no power over your sin. Let's briefly look at how unchecked sins might manifest themselves in a relationship or marriage. Selfishness can lead to abandonment. Pornography could result in adultery. Anger may turn into abuse. A lack of self-control can bring about financial ruin. These are but a few examples of sins that can lead to devastation within a relationship or marriage. If you want to become a "good" husband, you are going to need Christ's help. This is why it is vital that you establish a relationship with Christ before pursuing a woman.

Idols of the Heart

Let's take a moment to assess the condition of your heart. Do you feel discontent in your singleness? Is your life dominated by your search for the "One"? Are your thoughts and efforts completely consumed with your significant other? Take a moment to ask yourself, "What holds my heart captive?" When Jesus was tested by the Pharisees, He was asked, "Teacher, which is the great[est] commandment in the Law?' And He said to him, 'You shall love the Lord your God with all your heart and with all your soul and with all your mind'" (*Matthew 22:36-37*). God also commanded His people to not exalt idols above Him (*Exodus 20:3*). Do you realize that you worship what you love most? If your heart is dominated by anything other than a love for God, you have replaced Him with that idol of your heart. Your topmost priority should be developing a heart that is captivated with Christ.

Is Christ My Lord?

Take a brief moment to ask yourself, "Am I a Christian?" or "Is Jesus Christ truly Lord of my life?" If your answer is "no," "I don't know" or "maybe," then now is the time to start investigating what it means to be a child of God. Securing your eternal destiny is much more important than sorting out your romance life.

Don't you want God to lead you to the right spouse instead of doing it blindly by yourself? Romans 8:28 says, "And we know that God causes all things to work together for good to those who love God, to those who are called according to his purpose" (*NASB*). This promise is only for those who love and follow God. If you don't have a relationship with Him, there's no guarantee that He will bless your romantic pursuits.

Also, your Creator knows you more intimately than you could ever know yourself. Since that's true, don't you want His help in finding your "perfect match"? Prioritize securing your life in Him first. In doing so, you can rely on God to help you make one of the most important decisions of your life—choosing a spouse.

The Gospel Message

Mankind has a major problem. Romans 3:23 says, "[For] all have sinned and fall short of the glory of God ... " In addition, the Bible describes the human race as being "dead" in their sins (*Ephesians 2:1*). This means that we are incapable of having a relationship with God through our own strength. But here is the good news: John 3:16 says, "For God so loved the world, that he gave his only Son, that whoever believes in Him should not perish but have eternal life." This is the Gospel message. Christ was punished for our sins so that we might have the opportunity to spend eternity with Him.

How Can I Have a Relationship with God?

Romans 10:9 says, "... if you confess with your mouth that Jesus is Lord and believe in your heart that God raised him from the dead, you will be saved." If you repent of your sins, believe in Christ, and confess Him as Lord, you will enter into communion with the God of the universe. You can do this right now. Why wait? You are not guaranteed tomorrow. Today is the day of salvation!

"But I'm too Sinful ... God will Never Forgive Me"

You might think that you are beyond God's grace because of the sinful decisions you've made or are currently making. But if you're reading this now, it's not too late! Romans 10:13 says, "For 'everyone who calls on the name of the Lord will be saved.'" This means that *anyone* who asks for forgiveness, and invites Christ into their heart will receive pardon from eternal punishment. It doesn't matter what sins you've committed. Forgiveness is available to anyone who might receive it.

How Do I Know I'm a Christian?

Maybe you are someone who thinks that you're a Christian, but are not entirely sure. To better understand your spiritual state, think of all of the things that you hold dearest in life. Ask yourself, "Am I willing to give up any or all of these in order to have a relationship with God?" If your answer is "No" or "I'm not sure," then you should be concerned. Investigate why Christ is not "number one" in your life. As stated earlier, God asks you to love Him with your entire being.

1 John 1:6 says, "If we say that we have fellowship with him while we walk in darkness, we lie and do not practice the truth." Do you "walk in darkness" or love your sin? These are good questions to ask yourself to assess your spiritual condition. Be sure that your master is the God of the universe, and none other.

Concluding Thoughts

Hopefully, you now have a deeper understanding of the need for a right relationship with Christ before pursuing a soulmate. Your fellowship with God is the most vital relationship you will ever encounter. Everything else can wait.

Perhaps you still don't feel at peace after reading this chapter, and would like to ensure that Jesus Christ is your personal Savior. In that case, I encourage you to talk to a trusted pastor, church elder or other Christian that you know. This will be the most important decision that you'll ever make. Don't rest until you know you are secure in God's loving arms.

A Testimony of God's Grace

My father-in-law, Walt, is one of the most kind, loving, and God-centered men I know. I love spending time with him, because every time I see him I catch a fuller glimpse of who Christ is. As I reflect on Walt's testimony, I'm amazed at the radical transformation God allowed to take place in his life. I wish to share with you his salvation story to encourage you that you are never beyond God's grace. Regardless of your sin, God is patient, loving and forgiving. Here is Walt's testimony:

Like many young men, I tried to demonstrate my worth by being tough. Because my family relocated several times, I felt pressure to constantly prove myself in order to make friends. To compensate for my circumstances, I set out to show that I was meaner and tougher than the next guy. Competing in sports, mainly competitive wrestling, was one way to fit in with the crowd.

Always feeling the pressure to measure up to someone else's expectation, I wore the wounds of fighting with pride. A combination of pride and caving into peer pressure brought much heartache into my life. At an early age, I fell into alcohol abuse, which led to other serious offenses. By the time I graduated from high school, I left behind a trail of broken relationships and bad memories I wish I could forget. What lay ahead of me was an empty future with no plans, no opportunity, and little hope. I found myself alone wishing I was someone else.

I blamed my misery on my environment. So I decided to move up into the mountains to be a river-raft guide on the Colorado River. But my sinful nature followed me, and my self-destructive ways only intensified.

One morning, I stood waiting for rafting tourists to show up for a trip down the river. They were already two hours late, so I told my boss that I was just going to leave. Just then, a van drove down to the river landing, and out stepped an attractive, blonde girl. Sarcastically, I told my boss that I had a change of heart. We both laughed, but little did I know how crucial that moment would be for my future.

That day was the dawn of a new life for me. The woman in the van was more than just a cute girl. This was a woman who would challenge my misguided beliefs, and show me that my misery was a result of my own choices. Eventually, Judy would explain my need for Christ, and become my future wife.

While lying in bed one night, I reflected on what I heard in a church service that Judy once took me to. I recalled all the past wrongs I had done to myself and others. God convicted me with these words, “I was there and saw all that you did.” Somehow I knew I could not hide myself from the eyes of the One who made me. I had no other choice but to admit my guilt and accept my fate. Then God comforted me saying, “But I still love you.” I was conflicted. I kept asking myself, “If it was God who put those thoughts in my head, how could He love me even after all I’ve done?” That moment marked a turning point in my life. For the first time, I felt free of my past, and had hope for a brighter future.

Throughout the years, I came to a greater understanding of the forgiveness that God offered me. Gradually, I learned how to submit my life to my Maker, and realized that I could only reach my greatest stature while on my knees before God.

Eventually, I came to understand God’s purpose in everything that He had me go through. Matthew 16:25 says, “For whoever wishes to save his life will lose it; but whoever loses his life for my sake will find it” (*NASB*). I realized that I had to forsake all pride and selfishness, willfully give up my desires, and live solely for Christ.

As a new man, my life’s single purpose is to live for God. I now understand what it means to be reborn in His image. I am free of all past guilt and shame, and I can relate to the Apostle Paul who said:

I have been crucified with Christ. It is no longer I who live, but Christ who lives in me. And the life I now live in the flesh I live by faith in the Son of God, who loved me and gave himself for me.
- Galatians 2:20

Walt and Judy on their 25th Wedding Anniversary

"Trust in the Lord with all your heart... and He will make your paths straight."
- Proverbs 3:5-6 (NASB)

Personal Reflections

1. Why is developing a strong relationship with Christ more important than pursuing a romantic relationship?

2. Are there any "idols of the heart" hindering you from devoting yourself completely to Christ? What holds your heart captive?

3. Is Jesus Christ Lord of your life? If you're unsure, or know that you're not a Christian, what must you do to be saved?

CHAPTER 2

The Man to Become

"Don't let anyone look down on you because you are young, but set an example for the believers in speech, in conduct, in love, in faith and in purity."
- 1 Timothy 4:12 (NIV)

Before looking for the *right woman*, it's crucial to focus on becoming the *right man*. Otherwise, what do you have to offer? The amount of effort you put into refining your character now will significantly impact your future spouse. It's much better to develop character basics during your single years, than to struggle with them in marriage. In order to lead a wife, you must be able to lead your own life effectively.

A Man After God's Own Heart

God once said, " ... 'I have found in David the son of Jesse a man after my heart, who will do all my will'" (*Acts 13:22*). It is evident that David was a man who desired to fulfill God's will for his life. God used David in many mighty ways which included defeating a giant, winning battles, and becoming king of the Israelites.

Let's take a moment to look at your own heart. Can you be described as being "a man after God's own heart"? Do you have a desire to live your life in service to God's will? Or are your greatest efforts centered on your own ambitions?

It's important to prioritize a pursuit of God's will over a pursuit of a relationship. Jesus said, "But seek first the kingdom of God and his righteousness, and all these things will be added to you" (*Matthew 6:33*). It's clear that our first priority in life should be to seek to accomplish God's will. If we do so, we can take comfort in God's promise to provide all our needs.

Teachable-ness and Pride

Think about how difficult it would be to live with a stubborn or arrogant spouse. Imagine never "feeling heard" since your opinion isn't valued. Marital issues remain unresolved because your spouse is too prideful to own up to sin. This doesn't sound very appealing, does it? The fact is, any one of us can turn into this kind of spouse if we let pride control us. Do you have the potential to become this kind of person? Does pride have a grip on your heart?

A humble and teachable spirit must be instilled in the life of every believer if he or she expects to grow spiritually. Proverbs 12:15 says, "The way of a fool is right in his own eyes, but a wise man listens to advice." Do you humbly accept your parents' or elders' advice? Or can you be described as being "right in your own eyes?"

Even when you are convinced that you are right on an issue, it is important to temper your perspective with humility. 1 Corinthians 10:12 says, "Therefore let anyone who thinks that he stands take heed lest he fall." Sometimes our pride can blind us against truth, and the consequences can be quite devastating. It's important to begin fostering humility in your heart now. There is no rightful place for pride in the heart of a Christian. Becoming teachable will not only enrich your spiritual life, but it will also bless your future spouse.

Pursuing Wisdom

Later on, you may be called to lead a wife. In this case, you will have to make tough decisions, and know how to handle delicate situations with grace. Some examples might include: buying a home, resolving conflict between family members, dealing with sickness, and much more. In order to be an effective leader, you are going to need wisdom. Or, at the very least, you will need to know how to get it.

How does one begin to acquire wisdom? Proverbs 4:7 says, "The beginning of wisdom is this: Get wisdom, and whatever you get, get insight." The key to gaining wisdom is to simply go and get it! Scripture also says that we are to search for wisdom as "hidden treasure" (*Proverbs 2:4*). This means that finding it will require much effort.

Where can one find wisdom? Thankfully, God has provided us with a primary source of knowledge: His written Word. 2 Timothy 3:16-17 says, "All Scripture is breathed out by God and profitable for teaching, for reproof, for correction, and for training in righteousness, that the man of God may be complete, equipped for every good work." All you will ever need to know about leading a godly life can be found in the Bible.

Where else can wisdom be discovered? Proverbs 1:20 says, "Wisdom cries aloud in the street ... " This means that wisdom is clear and abundant! Just take a look around you. Observe the outcomes of others' good actions. Take note of the repercussions of bad decisions. There's a lot that can be learned from simply observing the people around you.

In addition, God has provided us with an abundance of resources. If you don't attend church, find one! Get to know your church leaders and fellow Christians. Read good books. Obtaining wisdom should be a priority in your life. One pastor put it this way: "You must constantly put yourself in the way of truth."[1]

---

[1] Holland, R. (1999, September 19). *The Recognition And Reality Of A Righteous Man Part 2 by Rick Holland.* Retrieved October 10, 2016, from Grace Community Church of the Valley: https://www.gracechurch.org/sermons/4993

Discipleship

Part of "pursuing wisdom" involves actively seeking counsel from older, godly men. Their wisdom will be especially valuable when looking for a spouse. Proverbs 15:22 says, "Without counsel plans fail, but with many advisers they succeed." It's critical to get outside opinions throughout your life. You won't always know all of life's answers, and may not see things clearly due to a lack of experience. So why not talk to those who are older than you? They possess a wealth of experience, and have witnessed the outcomes of their own and others' life choices. Take advantage of the opportunity to gain insight from wise men while you are still young.

The Fruit of the Spirit

Galatians 5:22-23 says, "But the fruit of the Spirit is love, joy, peace, patience, kindness, goodness, faithfulness, gentleness, self-control ... " Is your life characterized by peace? Or are you anxious? Are you kind to others? Or does your pride make life difficult for those around you? How about self-control? Does money always seem to be "burning a hole in your pocket"? You should actively refine the "fruit of the Spirit" in your life. These character traits are a lifelong pursuit, but they are foundational to becoming a godly future spouse.

Developing a Servant Mindset

A servant mindset is a key quality to possess as a future husband. Marriage is all about sacrifice. In Ephesians 5, the husband is commanded to selflessly love his wife in the same way that Christ loves His church (we will discuss this topic in more detail in a later chapter).

In what manner do you find yourself serving the Lord? Do you look for ways to help family members around the house? Do you meet the needs of those around you? Are you involved in church ministries? Colossians 3:23-24 says, "Whatever you do, work heartily, as for the Lord and not for men, knowing that from the Lord you will receive the inheritance as your reward. You are serving the Lord Christ." Once you find a way to serve, do as Paul says. "Work heartily"! Developing a servant mindset now will assist you in preparing to become a selfless husband.

Leadership and Firmness of Faith

God placed the responsibility of leadership on the husband (*Ephesians 5:22-23*). This quality is not something that can be learned overnight. You must begin acquiring leadership skills now in order to prepare for marriage.

1 Corinthians 16:13 says, "Be watchful, stand firm in the faith, act like men, be strong." Are you "strong"? Do you "stand firm in the faith" even when others don't? When your friends stray into trouble, are you easily persuaded to join them? We must learn to grow in faith, and " ... no longer be children, tossed to and fro by the waves and carried about by every wind of doctrine, by human cunning, by craftiness in deceitful schemes" (*Ephesians 4:14*).

Walking the "straight and narrow" can be a very lonely road at times. But, if your faithfulness endures, you'll experience the fruit of your labor. Eventually, your friends' popularity will disappear and their true substance will be revealed. Instead of "going with the crowd," be someone who stands out among your peers. Become a leader who influences others to do good rather than becoming easily influenced into foolishness yourself.

Concluding Thoughts

Humility, a pursuit of wisdom, the fruits of the Spirit, servanthood, and leadership are all key character traits that every woman should look for in a man. After reading this chapter, would you consider yourself to be an "attractive" potential spouse? In other words, are you "marriageable?" If you're hoping to start or continue in a relationship, it is important to instill these qualities in your own life.

Of course, no one can achieve complete perfection. We are certainly errant human beings with a sin nature. But God expects us to do our best to thrive in every one of these areas. Make it a priority to become the *right man*.

Lessons from a Prodigal

Because God loves us, He sometimes allows us go through difficult trials to train us to love what is good and right. This story is about how God used hardship to teach a close friend of mine the value of humbly seeking Him first.

When Jeremy [name changed] was a teenager, he seemed to have everything going for him. He was good-looking, popular, a talented musician, a snowboarder, and had a great sense of humor. He had everything he needed: a place to live, family, friends, and a good church. Beyond all this, Jeremy even developed an attachment to a girl from his church youth group.

Jeremy's attraction to this girl started out quite innocently. But, as time progressed, he began to develop an unhealthy obsession for the relationship. He lost sight of making Christ his first love, and allowed a false delusion of romance to dominate his life.

As this obsession became increasingly obvious, people began expressing their concerns to Jeremy. He was approached by friends, parents, and even church leaders. They warned him of the dangerous consequences of the direction in which he was headed. He was encouraged to regain the focus of making Christ his first love.

But Jeremy had already decided that he knew what was best. He chose to view the people who were trying to help him as mere hindrances in his pursuit of "love."

Friction escalated between Jeremy and his counselors, and his heart grew harder. As soon as he turned 18, he packed his bags, and left everything behind in order to pursue his fantasy. "Finally," Jeremy thought, "I'm free!" Nothing seemed to be stopping him. As a result, he freely continued down his path of obsession.

But one day it all came to an abrupt halt. One year after leaving home, Jeremy was shocked to discover that the girl he was interested in had developed affections for another man. His romantic fantasy had been shattered. He thought, "After all I sacrificed, how could this happen? I thought she was 'the one'!"

Shortly afterward, the relationship crumbled. Jeremy suddenly realized the miserable state of his current situation. He was living in a basement, and working a depressing overnight job, with no friends, no family, and no girlfriend. He had nothing. He then fell into depression, and began to hate his life. How could he have given up all that he had for a love that proved empty? Everything seemed lost to him.

The darkness grew deeper in Jeremy's life. He began to harm himself physically, and look for fulfillment in empty, worldly remedies to ease his pain.

Eventually, Jeremy could stand his life no longer. One night, he decided to end his misery. He left the cluttered basement he was living in, started his car, and drove to a nearby bridge. He scouted out the area, and identified a path wide enough for a car to fit through. He drove a little way down the road, turned his vehicle around, and began racing toward the bridge at full speed. Through the rain, music, tears, and pounding of his heart, he began yelling in terror. Then, for some reason, he slammed on the brakes and stopped just short of the bridge. Angrily, he got out of the car, looked toward the sky, and began yelling, "God! I hate my life! Why did you do this to me? How could you let this happen?" At that very moment, God planted a convicting thought into his mind, "You did this to yourself." Jeremy then realized that God was not responsible for his mistakes. He began to recount the many opportunities he had been given to repent in the past.

Jeremy then got back in his car, and went back to his bedroom. He recognized the sinful choices he had made in his life, and wanted to change things. Jeremy didn't even know where to begin! But he knew it would start with humility. So the first thing he did was call his father to seek forgiveness for rejecting his counsel.

This action was just the first step of humility. After that phone call, Jeremy spent much time restoring relationships, making apologies, uprooting sin, and seeking wisdom. Today, Jeremy continues to grow, and impact others through his testimony. He has even been blessed with a fiancée whom, Lord willing, he will marry someday.

This real-life example demonstrates the effects that a lack of teachable-ness can have on a person's life. Listen to the Proverb that states, "Do not be wise in your own eyes; fear the Lord and turn away from evil" (*Proverbs 3:7, NASB*). You don't have to relate with the remorseful man who said, "... How I have hated instruction! And my heart spurned reproof! I have not listened to the voice of my teachers, nor inclined my ear to my instructors!" (*Proverbs 5:12-13, NASB*).

If there is any pride in your heart, let this story be a wakeup call. Pride left unchecked will only increase in power over your life. Embrace humility, be selfless and pursue wisdom so that the Fruit of the Spirit may flourish in your life. Become the right man before pursuing the right woman.

Personal Reflections

1. In what areas do you see pride in your own life, and how can you work on becoming more teachable?

2. Why should you pursue wisdom, and how can you get it?

3. Would you consider yourself to be "firm" in your faith? What are some ways in which you can become a better leader?

CHAPTER 3

Contentment

"...for I have learned to be content in whatever circumstances I am. I know how to get along with humble means,
and I also know how to live in prosperity;
in any and every circumstance I have learned the secret of being filled and going hungry, both of having abundance and suffering need. I can do all things through Him who strengthens me."
- Philippians 4:11-13 (NASB)

Do you ever find yourself worrying about whether or not you'll get married someday? Are you someone who anxiously strives to maintain a relationship? If so, you should question where you are placing your trust and satisfaction. Contentment is essential whether you are single or in a relationship. When it comes to finding contentment, a good role model to look to is the Apostle Paul. He was a single man who found the "secret" to being content in "any and every circumstance." Take a brief moment to read over the passage at the beginning of this chapter. Did you know that Paul actually wrote that while he was in prison? How is it possible that he could display such contentment despite such afflicting circumstances? What is this "secret" that he spoke of? This chapter is devoted to answering that very question. It contains key principles and tools that will assist you on your journey to discovering complete and lasting fulfillment in Christ alone.

Trusting God

If you find yourself becoming anxious about relationships, you inadvertently doubt God's ability to provide for you. Proverbs 3:5-6 says, "Trust in the Lord with all your heart and do not lean on your own understanding. In all your ways acknowledge Him, and He will make your paths straight" (*NASB*). Notice that the author encourages you to put *all* your trust in God, and to depend on Him in *all* areas of your life. This includes relying on His provision for a spouse. He promises to secure your future if you only trust Him.

With this in mind, hold onto your cares loosely. Let God be the One Who takes control. Since God promises to work out everything for your good (*Romans 8:28*), why not trust Him? Have confidence in the Lord even when circumstances don't make sense at the time. Have the same attitude as Job. After tragically losing all his children and belongings, he still was able to say, " ... the Lord gave, and the Lord has taken away; blessed be the name of the Lord" (*Job 1:21*). When placing your trust in Him, you lay a foundation in which you can begin to learn the "secret" of contentment.

Delighting in God

So what is Paul's "secret"? How does one attain contentment? The answer is found in Psalm 37:4. It says, "Delight yourself in the Lord, and He will give you the desires of your heart." Delighting in God is the act of experiencing the fulfillment and joy that naturally comes through fostering an intimate relationship with Him. When you loosen your grasp on your own ambitions and become attuned to God's will, your desires will begin to mold to His. In doing so, you will discover His promise of true and everlasting contentment.

Serving God

Do you ever drift into loneliness or depression due to singleness? Perhaps you feel empty after discovering that true happiness cannot be found in a woman. A wise person once told me, "The cure for depression is to get up and serve someone." When serving others, naturally, your mind is taken off of yourself. You keep busy by tending to the needs of others, thus fulfilling God's command to "love one another" (*John 13:34*). In addition, you experience the joyful satisfaction that is found in leaving a positive impact on someone else's life. As Jesus said, " ... 'it is more blessed to give than to receive'" (*Acts 20:35*).

There are endless opportunities to reach out to those around you. Start off by getting to know people. Ask, "How can I pray for you?" If you know someone who is going through a hard time, find a way to encourage them. If you see someone who looks lonely, sit by them! Don't waste your time wishing that you were in a relationship when you could be giving your "undivided devotion to the Lord" in your singleness (*1 Corinthians 7:32-35*). Become so distracted with serving that you have little time to think about yourself. Put on the mindset described by Paul: "Be devoted to one another in brotherly love; give preference to one another in honor; not lagging behind in diligence, fervent in spirit, serving the Lord ... " (*Romans 12:10-11, NASB*). Make a difference in your life by making a difference in someone else's.

Know the Goodness of the Lord

Do you ever wonder if God truly cares about your desires for a soulmate? Have you become frustrated with your singleness? Psalm 84:11 says, " ... No good thing does He withhold from those who walk uprightly." You can rest assured that if you abide by His Word, and in His Word, He will lovingly provide you with what is best for you. Now, God may very well have a life of singleness planned for you. Or He may have a special someone for you, but the timing isn't right. Perhaps He wants to teach you (or her) something first. Remember, you can only see a small part of God's greater plan. Your Creator knows you more intimately than anyone. Whether you stay single or get married, He will certainly give you every good thing He has planned for you.

Pray to the Lord

Many times, young men battle anxiety when it comes to relationships. Worries over singleness or ending up with a specific girl can be overwhelming. Have you felt this way lately? Philippians 4:6-7 says:

"Do not be anxious about anything, but in everything by prayer and supplication with thanksgiving let your requests be made known to God. And the peace of God, which surpasses all understanding, will guard your hearts and your minds in Christ Jesus."

This passage encourages you to surrender all your worries to the Lord. If you do so, God promises to provide an incomprehensible peace that will out-shadow any circumstance. What a wonderful promise to rest in.

You might ask, "But what if God doesn't answer my prayer?" The reality is that God answers prayer *all* of the time. His answer may be "Yes"; His answer may be "No"; and His answer might be "Wait." I'd like to add that God might even say, "Yes, but we will do it My way." His answer may not be exactly what you envision, but God has a much grander (and better!) plan in store for us. Don't spend another moment worrying about the future. Bring your cares to God in prayer, and experience His promised peace.

Contentment Found Only in the Lord

When I was young, I was told many times, "If you're not content as a single person, you won't be content as a spouse." As wonderful and fulfilling as my wife is, I've come to the realization that it's impossible to experience complete satisfaction if Christ is not my first love. Don't buy Satan's lie that "if you only had a girlfriend, then you'd be happy." The fact is that the person you will eventually pursue or marry is imperfect. It's unfair to expect her to be what only Christ can fulfill. Place your contentment in Christ alone by making Him your *first* love.

A Journey to Discovering True Contentment

In my high school years, I struggled with insecurity. It seemed as if everyone else my age had a girlfriend. I let peer pressure influence me to try and fit in with the popular group. Unfortunately, I caved in and forced my way into a "crush." Even though I was pure physically, I was failing emotionally and spiritually. I was so desperate that I ignored the Spirit's convicting call and advice from others. I began striving to maintain something that wasn't God's will for me.

As time went on, I became quite lonely, miserable, and depressed. I even recall losing the will to live. I knew that this lack of hope was not characteristic of a genuine Christian. Eventually, I couldn't bear the agony any longer. I got down on my knees, weeping, and pleaded with God. I still recall my prayer: "Lord, show me why I am so miserable! Remove whatever the obstacle is. I am willing to let go of anything even if it means being single. I want to serve You joyously again." After praying, an overwhelming sense of peace came over me. It was similar to the feeling I experienced the day Christ became my Savior.

Within just a few weeks, the situation that I had been forcing for years crumbled before my eyes. Strangely, I watched it all happen in complete peace even as drama erupted around me. I could have peace because I knew that I was no longer forcing my way in life, and that God had become my Guide. That moment marked the beginning of true spiritual traction in my life. I finally began to understand what it meant to find contentment in Christ alone.

Concluding Thoughts

Hopefully, you understand by now that true fulfillment is not found in a woman. The 'secret' of contentment can be discovered by resting your desires in God's hands and delighting in Him. You will not find complete satisfaction anywhere else. Recall Paul's example of contentment while in prison. Stop striving and place your complete trust in God, and let an inexplicable sense of peace overtake your heart. This is how you know that you are fulfilling God's will for your life. Trust, delight, serve, and pray. These are key elements to discovering true contentment in Christ.

Personal Reflections

1. In what areas do you find yourself becoming discontent or anxious?

2. What are some Biblical principles you can apply to overcome these struggles?

3. Why does delighting in God produce contentment?

CHAPTER 4

Establishing Purity

"How can a young man keep his way pure?
By guarding it according to your word."
- Psalm 119:9

Whether you' are single or in a relationship, it is important to realize the impact that purity can have on your future. Eventually, you will become "one" with your spouse. You will have to be honest about your past, and the truth may either cause hurt or it may bring joy.

A common misunderstanding is that a man's emotional and sexual battles end on the wedding day. You would be surprised at just how many husbands struggle with pornography. Maintaining purity doesn't stop at the altar. It's a lifelong pursuit that begins now.

Purity involves waiting for what is *good for you*. Since marital sex and intimacy are God's inventions, they truly are good things. Settling for cheap substitutes (such as flirtation, pornography, self-stimulation, or pre-marital sex) may seem enjoyable for a short time, but ultimately, they will not provide satisfaction.

This chapter will help you develop a frame-of-mind centered on reserving yourself physically, mentally, and emotionally for marriage. If you feel as if you are failing, don't be discouraged! You can start making changes today. Together, let's take a serious look at what it means to pursue purity.

God Forgives

An important first step in pursuing purity is to understand that God is *forgiving*. Perhaps you feel as if you are "beyond God's grace" or that "it's too late" for you because of your sin. Don't be deceived! This is just what Satan wants you to believe. He wants to prevent you from experiencing the unconditional grace that God has to offer. 1 John 1:9 says, "If we confess our sins, He is faithful and righteous to forgive us our sins and to cleanse us from all unrighteousness." The key word in this verse is "all." If you have asked for God's forgiveness, and if Christ is your Savior, you are free from *all* condemnation regardless of what you've done! Christ's sacrifice on the cross paid for your past, present, and future sins. Freedom is found in Christ! And forgiveness is a continual offer.

No Excuses

Now that we understand that we are free in Christ, let's take a look at how our pursuit of purity might be hindered if we try to justify our sin. In my youth, I used to excuse my sin by thinking, "It's just too hard for me to be pure since I'm single. Things will get better once I'm married. Besides, I'm just too busy to focus on purity!" My perspective changed dramatically when I realized that there was *no* excuse for my sin, and that I was accountable to God for my actions regardless of my circumstances. 1 Corinthians 10:13 says:

> *"No temptation has overtaken you that is not common to man. God is faithful, and he will not let you be tempted beyond your ability, but with the temptation he will also provide the way of escape, that you may be able to endure it."*

If you are a Christian, God has given you the ability to withstand any temptation through the Holy Spirit. With this knowledge, our outlook toward purity must change. We can no longer justify our sin by blaming it on anything outside of ourselves.

Being Honest About Our Sin

It's easy to fall into the trap of ignoring sin in our lives by convincing ourselves that we don't have a problem. I even recall times where I would judge others for the very same sins that I was struggling with. Why does this happen? The simple answer is pride. Naturally, we don't want to admit that we are flawed. We want to view ourselves as being "above" certain behaviors. But if we ever expect to grow spiritually, we must first be humble. James 4:6 admonishes us saying, " ... 'God opposes the proud, but gives grace to the humble.'" We have to be honest about our struggles by humbly recognizing our faults and confessing them to the Lord. Otherwise, our sin will only continue to grow in power over us.

Secondly, we should be humble and honest with others. Unfortunately, many men keep their sin to themselves and begin to feel alone in their struggle. They think, "I must be the only one with this problem." But keeping sin to ourselves is not healthy. James 5:16 instructs us to "confess [our] sins to one another". We should seek out and confide in trustworthy individuals. Of course, it can be quite intimidating to be open and vulnerable with someone about our sin! But I can honestly say that each time I've humbled myself in this manner, I've experienced the same grace mentioned in James 4:6. God always blesses a humble heart.

Bodily Purity

Let's turn our focus to understanding God's desire for physical purity. Many men lack the tools and knowledge needed to develop a proper perspective toward sexuality. They are often left wondering what is acceptable and what is not. A common question is, "Is it okay for me to do things with my body or view images as long as it doesn't affect others?" Outside of marriage, God's desire is for us to control *all* sexual passion.

The following passage will help us define proper boundaries around this subject. 1 Thessalonians 4:3-5 says:

> *"For this is the will of God, your sanctification: that you abstain from sexual immorality; that each one of you know how to control his own body in holiness and honor, not in the passion of lust like the Gentiles [unbelievers] who do not know God."*

Furthermore, control over sexual passion is especially vital if you are a Christian. Scripture compares the believer's body to a temple that houses God's Holy Spirit. 1 Corinthians 6:18-20 says:

> *"Flee from sexual immorality. Every other sin a person commits is outside the body, but the sexually immoral person sins against his own body. Or do you not know that your body is a temple of the Holy Spirit within you, whom you have from God? You are not your own, for you were bought with a price. So glorify God in your body."*

As priests were careful to follow God's precise instructions in the temple, we must have the same attitude concerning how we handle our bodies. If we commit sexual sin, we defile God's "house" since the Holy Spirit lives within us. Since our bodies belong to the Lord, let's carry out God's will for our lives by handling our sexuality with extreme care.

At this point, you may be wondering, "What is God's reason for wanting me to abstain from sexual sin?" The answer is that God desires for you to honor His design for marriage. Hebrews 13:4 says, "Let marriage be held in honor among all, and let the marriage bed be undefiled, for God will judge the sexually immoral and adulterous." Sexuality is something to be reserved for your wife only. *Any* sensual act committed outside of marriage is in violation of God's will and design.

Are you feeling the weight of everything you've just read? Maintaining sexual purity is obviously a significant challenge! But I'd like to encourage you with the reminder that God forgives, and that He will meet you wherever you're at in your pursuit of purity. I am quite certain that no man (besides Jesus) has ever been able to handle himself in complete sexual perfection. Take that feeling of discouragement and turn it into something positive: a hopeful challenge. Let's take a look at a few ways in which we can begin to gain control over our sexual passions. Romans 13:13-14 says:

> *"Let us behave properly as in the day, not in carousing and drunkenness, not in sexual promiscuity and sensuality, not in strife and jealousy. But put on the Lord Jesus Christ, and make no provision for the flesh in regard to its lusts." (Emphasis added, NASB)*

We are instructed to not give sin an opportunity to take place in our lives. Certainly, we aren't able to control everything we encounter in life. But we must do our best to guard ourselves against anything that could cause us to stumble. Are you careful about what you see? (Videos, images, immodesty) Do you filter what you hear? (Music, language, filthy jokes) Do you avoid environments or situations that might bring temptation? (Worldly parties, late nights with the opposite sex) These are all areas that could become potential "opportunities for the flesh." Be wise about what you allow yourself to be exposed to.

In addition, it is helpful to remind yourself that God is with you at all times. Satan often whispers lies to us saying, "Go ahead. Do it. There won't be any consequences. You can hide it." On the contrary, Scripture is clear that nothing is hidden from God. Proverbs 15:3 says, "The eyes of the Lord are in every place, watching the evil and the good" (*NASB*). If we truly believed this, how could we ever bring ourselves to sin sexually right in front of God? It's a convicting thought.

Purity of the Heart

Purity involves much more than simply refraining from sinful "touch." Jesus said in Matthew 5:27-28, "You have heard that it was said, 'You shall not commit adultery'; but I say to you that everyone who looks at a woman with lust for her has already committed adultery with her in his heart" (*NASB*). Have you ever treated lust as a "lesser sin?" According to Jesus, it's just as bad as committing physical adultery. Since sin originates from the heart, and thus affects our actions, we should place a high priority on purifying our hearts and minds.

Let's take purity of the heart one step further. What dominates your thought-life? Is your mind consumed with thoughts about a romantic partner? Do you find yourself allowing your heart to become infatuated with woman after woman? God has made it clear for us to "have no other gods before [Him]" (*Exodus 20:3*), and to love Him with all of our heart, mind, soul and strength (*Luke 10:27*). If anything has dominion over your heart, you are in fact worshiping it. Pursuing purity involves ridding ourselves of the "idols of the heart," and replacing them with a love for God.

Sowing to the Spirit

Is the battle against lust difficult for you? Perhaps you feel discouraged after giving into temptation time and time again. Fortunately, Scripture explains why this is the case, and offers a solution to gaining true spiritual traction. Galatians 6:8 says:

> *"For the one who sows to his own flesh will from the flesh reap corruption, but the one who sows to the Spirit will from the Spirit reap eternal life."*

This passage uses farming as an analogy to illustrate this principle: you get what you plant or, more commonly said, "You reap what you sow." If you plant an apple seed, you will most definitely get an apple tree. The same principle can be applied to your spiritual life. If you entertain sinful seeds, your life will yield sin. On the other hand, if you plant righteous seeds, you will reap righteousness. A simple way to understand this principle is this: if you don't want a sin "plant," don't plant a sin "seed."

So, what do "seeds of corruption" look like, and how can we avoid them? Let's take a brief moment to examine your daily life. What kind of movies do you watch? Are they filled with sexuality? Do you listen to music containing subtle themes that make sin seem okay? What content are you allowing yourself to be exposed to through video games? These are just a few examples of areas that could contain "seeds of corruption."

As you can see, it's extremely important to be careful about what seeds we plant in our lives. So, instead of sowing sinful seeds, plant seeds that will grow into the "fruits of the Spirit" (*Galatians 5:22-23*). You can do this by reading Scripture, communing with God through prayer, and abiding by the following passage. Philippians 4:8 says:

> *"Finally, brothers, whatever is true, whatever is honorable, whatever is just, whatever is pure, whatever is lovely, whatever is commendable, if there is any excellence, if there is anything worthy of praise, think about these things."*

Devote yourself to dwelling on anything that is "worthy of praise." Maybe this involves immersing yourself in truthful teachings, godly friends, or uplifting songs! If you make God the center of your daily life, you will most certainly see the effects of righteousness take place in your heart.

Concluding Thoughts

Hopefully, you have a greater recognition of the importance of purity, and feel more equipped on how to pursue it. By dealing with sin now and embracing righteousness, you will be more effective at bringing God glory, both as a single and as a future spouse. We need to pursue purity.

In my youth, I had always viewed myself as a "good person." But, at an early age, that perception was shattered. As my father uncovered hidden sin in my life, I was forced to recognize who I truly was: a sinner in desperate need of grace. That was the moment I asked for God's forgiveness, and asked Jesus to become Lord of my life.

Even though my heart was transformed, I was still plagued by my sin nature. Purity was a battle all throughout my teen years, and I had a hard time understanding why.

During a particularly difficult time in my life, I finally gathered the courage to seek help from a trusted church elder. It was then that I came to understand that the battle for purity was lost long before an act was ever committed. I realized that I needed to do some "weeding" in my heart and mind, and start "planting seeds" of righteousness. I reevaluated the sinful influences in my life, and, most importantly, became proactive in prayer and planting God's Word in my heart.

Eventually, I noticed that temptation became less prevalent in my life. The battles still existed, but the temptations seemed less overpowering. It was much easier to overcome sin through Christ's power rather than my own strength.

I'm now married, but I still have to apply this same principle to my life daily. Temptations become greater when entertaining sinful influences, but sin loses its power when embracing godliness.

The Lord requires us to "weed" sin and to "plant" righteousness. If we do this, He will surely sustain us. "How can a young man keep his way pure? By guarding it according to your word" (*Psalm 119:9*).

Personal Reflections

1. What are some ways you might be justifying or excusing why you fall into temptation?

2. What are some "seeds of corruption" that might be preventing you from thriving in purity?

3. What are some ways in which you can start cultivating righteousness in your life?

CHAPTER 5

Practical Preparations

"Commit your works to the Lord
and your plans will be established."
- Proverbs 16:3 (NASB)

As you determine whether or not you're ready for a relationship, it's important to assess your ability to support a family. Ask yourself, "Do I have a plan for becoming the provider that God wants me to be? If so, am I making progress in this area?" This chapter is devoted to exploring this topic by assessing age, career, and financial readiness. These are all important factors to consider since they significantly impact your ability to provide for a future family.

Age Appropriateness

Have you ever heard someone say, "I'm almost old enough to date!"? Turning 16 (or whatever society determines as the "benchmark" age) does not necessarily mean that you're ready for a relationship. You could be 30 years old and still not mature enough to be a husband. On the other hand, you may be an independent 21-year-old who's already in a position to effectively care for a family. Since age alone is not the best determiner of relationship readiness, choose to focus more on assessing your spiritual and practical maturity.

Certainly, age may need to be considered. For instance, it's wise to maintain a healthy amount of distrust in the emotions that you and your peers experience during your teen years. Many teenagers mistake their fluctuating hormones as "God's voice" influencing them to pursue a girl. It's important to seek guidance from more mature (i.e., older), godly men to help you develop discernment during your youth.

You may be wondering, "So how long will it be before I'm ready for a relationship?" Let's take a moment to estimate this by doing a quick (and easy!) math problem.

Write the age you think you'd be "marriage-ready": (a) _____

Write your current age: (b) _____

Now, calculate the difference: (a) – (b) = _____

The number of years you calculated is an estimate of how long you would have to wait before you're ready to be married. Does your answer surprise you? It will be good to ask yourself this question: "If I started a relationship now, would my wait until marriage be too long or drawn-out?" In other words, how much opportunity is there for stress, temptation, or complexity to arise due to the wait? Hopefully, this assessment will help you determine whether or not you're even close to being ready for a relationship.

Understanding Your Future Role

The next important topic to consider is your future role as a provider. God has given men the important responsibility of supplying their family's material and financial needs. 1 Timothy 5:8 says:

> *"But if anyone does not provide for his relatives, and especially for members of his household, he has denied the faith and is worse than an unbeliever."*

Notice the intensity of the verbiage in the passage above. A man who willfully neglects his duty to provide for his family is considered "worse than an unbeliever." This instruction should create a sense of urgency within you. It's time to be responsible by thoughtfully preparing for your future role.

It is also wise to prepare yourself to become the *sole* provider of your household. Certainly, it's not sinful for a wife to work. In some cases, it may make perfect sense for her to maintain a job. For instance, many newlywed couples start out dependent upon two incomes. But complexities often arise when children become a factor. Some people become unexpectedly pregnant. Others have convictions against the use of contraceptives. And some simply desire to begin a family. Unfortunately, being dependent upon two incomes presents a few problems. In order to make ends meet, your wife may be forced to maintain her job. This could potentially interfere with her God-given role of caring for her family (this topic will be expounded upon in a later chapter). Or perhaps, in order to let your wife stay at home, you would have to work multiple jobs. This would likely divert much of your time and energy away from the family. Therefore, it's wise to pursue a career that would enable you to sufficiently provide independent of your wife's income. In doing so, God is honored through your efforts to minimize obstacles which could impose on your familial responsibilities.

Be Diligent in Planning Your Career

In order to become a provider, you will need a path to get there. Let's take a moment to discuss the importance of responsibly planning your future career.

Unfortunately, many young men are not diligent in defining their career pursuits. Some let indecisiveness cause them to overstay their time in college as they accrue large debts. Others aimlessly choose an educational path without much thought or research. As a result of this kind of behavior, much time and money is wasted. Proverbs 10:4 says, "A slack hand causes poverty, but the hand of the diligent makes rich." Also, Proverbs 21:5 says, "The plans of the diligent lead surely to abundance, but everyone who is hasty comes only to poverty." When you're in your teens or twenties, it's important to be neither negligent nor hasty about defining your future career.

It is also important to proactively assess what quality of life you want your future family to have *before* pursuing a career. Do yourself a favor by researching the average wages associated with specific majors and trades. Begin to ask yourself some of the following questions:

- How much money will I need to earn?
- How many kids do I want to have?
- What are my convictions on "family planning"?
- Will I need a big house or a small house?
- Will I need a small car or a van?
- How many jobs am I willing to work?
- What if my future wife has different convictions from mine?

These types of questions will help define what kind of career you should (or shouldn't) pursue. Be diligent by preparing for your future career now.

Your Career is Not About You

Next, it's important to not fall into the trap of pursuing a career solely for self-fulfillment. Too many men become consumed with their jobs and neglect their families. Certainly, it's important to pursue a path that you don't despise. However, your main reason for having a job should be to bring God glory. Colossians 3:23-24 says:

> *"Whatever you do, work heartily, as for the Lord and not for men, knowing that from the Lord you*

will receive the inheritance as your reward. You are serving the Lord Christ."

There are many ways you can bring glory to God through your work. You can provide for your family, give to charity, share the Gospel with your coworkers, and more! Remember to not make your career about you. Rather, use it for God's glory.

Financial Stewardship

As a future provider, you will have to interact, in at least some way, with finances. Let's look at some character qualities that will enable you to become a better financial leader.

Let's first talk about debt. As important as it is to obtain an education, house, vehicle, etc. it's also important that you don't drown yourself in unrepayable loans and credit cards. Imagine the financial burden you'd bring into your marriage if you had tens of thousands of dollars of debt tied to your name. Instead of putting your hard-earned money toward supporting your family, your income would get devoured by bills. Proverbs 22:7 says, "The rich rule over the poor, and the borrower is slave to the lender" (*NIV*). Don't become a "slave" to debt. This weight will impose stress on both you and your family. Many studies show that financial pressures are listed among the leading causes of divorce. Avoid unneeded financial stress by doing everything you can to evade and eliminate debt.

It is also crucial to learn how to handle your money wisely. Proverbs 3:9 says, "Honor the Lord with your wealth and with the first fruits of all your produce." Your money is not yours; rather, it's the Lord's. As God's money-handler, have you been proactive in learning the basics about budgeting and saving? Since one of the "fruits of the Spirit" is "self-control," have you developed the willpower to say "no" to frivolous spending? Or do you find it hard to turn down that game, movie, restaurant, etc.? Learn how to become responsible with your money now so that you will be better prepared to handle finances as a married man.

Concluding Thoughts

Now that you've completed this chapter, go back to the small math problem that you did earlier. Take a moment to reassess how long it will be before you could consider yourself to be "marriage-ready."

Take these practical preparations seriously. It's your duty to provide for your future family. Don't earn the title of being "worse than an unbeliever" through laziness or negligence. Set a good foundation for your future now. Remember, every day that goes by is a day closer to your future marriage.

If you are looking for additional guidance on the topic of pursuing a career, an extra section is included in the Appendices for your reference.

A Personal Note

In order to bring the concepts discussed in this chapter to life, I thought I would share my own story. My personal experience should not be looked at as being the "ideal" model. Rather, I hope my own path encourages you to see that it is very possible to become a provider if you take your career seriously.

First, let me say, I never considered myself to be "naturally smart." In order to keep up with others around me, I had to work very hard. But I knew that I wanted to get married someday. This meant that I would need to put a lot of effort into obtaining an education.

So at age 16, I enrolled in a two-year government-funded program which allowed high school students to earn college credit. I knew that I didn't want to waste time or money deciding on what career to pursue, so I took introductory courses in fields that interested me. By the time I completed the program, I discovered that I had an aptitude for engineering.

At age 18, I enrolled in a two-year engineering transfer program at a community college. This seemed to be the cheapest yet most effective option at the time.

I then transferred my engineering credits over to a major university at age 20. During my senior year of college, God introduced me to the woman I would eventually marry.

After completing my degree at age 22, I moved out of the house, got a job and got engaged. A year later, by God's grace, I married my beautiful wife, and paid off the remainder of the $32,000 I had in student loans.

All throughout my college experience, I did my best to keep costs low by choosing less-expensive education, living with my parents, and working multiple jobs. Since I chose a career that promised to pay well, I was able to pay off school loans quickly. By the time I graduated, I was in a position to provide for a family independent of my wife's income. Having a career in place allowed for a shorter pre-engagement relationship and engagement. That helped reduce temptations that can often arise from prolonged waiting. In addition, we had a good running start to our marriage, with the freedom and resources to start our own family.

I can't end this story without stating the fact that I deserve no credit for my success. It was God alone who graciously allowed for a smooth transition from singleness to marriage. He provided the resources, advisors, and circumstances which helped many of the details to fall into place.

It is important to note that your own path may look very different than mine, and that is completely okay. Don't be discouraged if your career doesn't pan out smoothly! God has a unique plan for you, and will bless your obedience and diligence. Be encouraged by focusing on this truth: "Commit your works to the Lord and your plans will be established" (*Proverbs 16:3*).

Personal Reflections

1. How close are you to being "marriage-ready"? What do you need to accomplish in order to reach this goal?

2. Why is it important to be diligent in planning your future career?

3. What can you do now to prepare for your future role as a provider?

CHAPTER 6

Helping Your Fellow Sisters

"Treat ... younger women as sisters, with absolute purity."
- 1 Timothy 5:1-2 (NIV)

Often times, women are instructed on how they can help reduce temptations for men. Specifically, they're told what clothing to wear, and how they should act. But there seems to be a significant lack of focus on how we, as men, can help our fellow sisters in their own journey toward purity. Paul encouraged Timothy to " ... treat ... younger women as sisters, with absolute purity" (*1 Timothy 5:1-2*). My hope is that this chapter encourages you to help the single women around you to guard themselves for their future husbands.

Understanding a Woman's Gift of Emotion

In order to treat your fellow sisters with "absolute purity," it's important to gain a window into the female mind. Certainly, as a male, I do not claim to be an expert on the female psyche. So I have sought out much help from my wife, various books, and trusted counselors on this topic. My hope is to provide you with some basics in order to enable you to help your fellow sisters.

First, you must realize that women are truly different from us men, not just biologically, but *emotionally*. The unique emotions God has given them are a *gift*! God had a very special reason for creating women the way they are. Think for a moment about how mothers, in general, seem to have a natural gift for showing tenderness toward their children. Many women are uniquely sensitive and attuned to their feelings, and often, that of others. God created women the way they are to be man's "complement" in order to enrich areas where men may, generally, be less gifted.

A Gift Unbalanced

Unfortunately, ever since The Fall of mankind, this gift of emotion can become corrupted by sin. Some girls allow a craving for attention and emotional fulfillment to drive them to forsake a marriage mindset, and become "boy crazy." Other women might also be tempted to let their emotions control them, resulting in sins such as fear, anxiety, or insecurity. Because this is true, it is important to treasure your fellow sisters, and not give them reason to fall into these sins.

She Must Guard Her Heart

Just as you are encouraged to guard your heart, girls must be careful to guard theirs as well. Proverbs 4:23 says, "Watch over your heart with all diligence, for from it flow the springs of life" (*NASB*). It is important to keep this in mind when you interact with young ladies. Instead of giving them reasons to stumble emotionally, make it a priority to encourage them to guard their hearts.

Help Her by Not Flirting

Now that you know more about how a woman should guard her heart, let's take a look at what we, as men, can do to help them. Take a moment to assess how you interact with the ladies around you. Do you ever "innocently" flirt with them? Flirtation is reckless behavior. Hinting or expressing interest without serious intent does not help girls reserve their hearts for their future husbands. Consider this for a moment. What if you never marry her? What if God intends for your buddy, Joe, to become her "knight in shining armor?" Since God desires for a woman to reserve herself for marriage, don't shallowly toy around with her heart. Instead learn to interact with her as you would a sister (*1 Timothy 5:1-2*).

In addition, if you flirt with a girl, but are not serious about pursuing her for marriage, you are in fact defrauding her. You mislead her to believe that you have a sincere interest in her when, actually, you don't. This form of flirtation is plain deception. Deception is not "innocent," rather it is sin. Proverbs 12:22 says, "The Lord detests lying lips, but he delights in those who tell the truth" (*NLT*).

As a final note, I strongly encourage you to beware of making a habit out of flirting. Your habits quite easily carry over into adulthood, and this particular sin destroys marriages. In order to prepare yourself to be a faithful husband, deal honestly with your fellow sisters by not flirting.

Avoid Becoming Too Emotionally Involved

Girls can also be tempted to compromise if they become too emotionally involved with someone of the opposite sex. When talking to a girl, keep the conversations at a "high level." Don't become each other's "accountability partners." Just be a friend to her without purposefully prying into her emotions. If she's struggling, find an older, wiser woman who can disciple her. Respect her by conversing with her in a way that does not cause her to stumble.

Putting Up Physical Boundaries

For some girls, physical touch can cause them to struggle with emotional purity. It's important to interact with them in a way that does not compromise their ability to effectively guard their hearts.

Also, take a moment to recognize the fact that when you give a girl a hug, you are actually hugging a female body. Her body must be respected since it is something that should be reserved for her husband only. Certainly, I'm not saying that hugs are a bad thing or shouldn't be done. All I'm saying is that that you should be cautious about how "loose" you are when it comes to having physical contact with women.

Valuing a Woman's True Worth

A woman loses all respect for a man who objectifies her. Don't be interested in a lady merely because of her looks. She wants to feel valued for more than her body. She is a living soul with feelings, a personality, and qualities that she desires to be appreciated. Don't objectify her and make her feel as if her worth consists only in the way she looks.

Think of the Future

All too often, men don't realize that their present actions toward women can impact the quality of their future friendships. How you interact with girls early on can either produce healthy friendships or awkwardness. Many men I know are no longer able to have normal friendships with girls who are now their "ex-crushes" or "ex-girlfriends." After getting engaged or married, friendship with past girlfriends may become overwhelmingly awkward for everyone involved, especially if there was physical involvement. Imagine introducing an "ex-crush" to your future wife. Or think about how you would feel if your future wife introduced her ex-boyfriend to you. It doesn't sound too comfortable, does it? These situations often produce jealously, hurt, and broken relationships. If you haven't handled yourself well in the past, God forgives. What matters now is how you handle yourself going forward.

With these thoughts in mind, think about the friendships you have right now with the women around you. Would it eventually become awkward if you had to introduce your female friend to your future wife? Would it be difficult to maintain a friendship with these girls if you had a fiancée? Here is a good question to ask yourself: "Would my future wife be comfortable with the way that I'm interacting with my female friend?"

Self-checks: Am I Treating Her with Purity?

Here are a couple quick tips that can help you treat your fellow sisters in "absolute purity:"

- When speaking to a girl, ask, "Why am I talking to her? Is it because she's the prettiest face in the room? Or is it because I simply want to be friends?"
- If you find yourself sharing your struggles with a girl, ask yourself, "Am I doing this just to get attention from her?"
- Never assume that she has a romantic interest in you unless she has told you so.
- Treat all young ladies as someone else's future spouse—even if you are interested in them.
- Encourage her to guard her heart. Wouldn't you hope that other men are encouraging your future wife to do the same?

Treasuring a Fellow Sister

One of the major benefits of being married is that you get to know the other gender. You become aware of a whole new world of thinking. Soon after entering into a relationship with my wife, I recognized very quickly that she had a strong desire to guard her heart for her future husband. I was struck with the delicateness of how I should be handling myself around her considering that she wasn't truly "mine" yet. I realized that I could potentially be dating someone else's future spouse. As a result, I felt a responsibility to encourage her to constantly guard her heart.

Once we got engaged, those walls that she had built up started breaking down. Her heart started becoming emotionally attached. Later, she revealed to me that I was the first man that she had ever given her heart to. Although this wasn't an expectation of mine, her guardedness was and is still so precious to me. To think, she had me in mind all these years without even knowing who I was.

She now tells me often that she appreciates that I didn't push her to stumble emotionally. She treasures how I made it easier on her to reserve herself for her future husband (which ended up being me!).

Mandy has told me many times that she also treasures how I reserved her body for marriage. We enjoyed the sweetness of sharing our first kiss at the altar. Since I respected her body, she realized that I loved her beyond just the physical, and that she was far more than just an object. Rather she was and still is a woman to be treasured.

Personal Reflections

1. How are female emotions a gift, and how might they become unbalanced?

2. Why is it important for a girl to guard her heart?

3. What are some ways in which you can help the women you know to guard their hearts?

CHAPTER 7

Rethinking "Love"

"Love is patient and kind; love does not envy or boast; it is not arrogant or rude. It does not insist on its own way; it is not irritable or resentful; it does not rejoice at wrongdoing, but rejoices with the truth. Love bears all things, believes all things, hopes all things, endures all things. Love never ends ... "
- 1 Corinthians 13:4-8

What do you think of when you hear the word "love?" This word has been used in so many different ways. Sometimes it's used to describe how much someone enjoys an activity: "I love football!" Other times it's used to show affection between family or friends: "I love my brother." It also can be used to express romantic infatuation: "I love you." Notice that each of these examples use the same word, but have quite different meanings. Unfortunately, the word "love" often gets thrown around too lightly. Typically, people use the word to express an emotion that they are feeling at the moment, but don't understand its true depth. This chapter is devoted to helping you develop a deeper definition of what "love" truly is, and how you can live it out in your own life.

A Misguided Definition of "Love"

Before jumping in too deeply, let's look at a common imbalance that the film industry has presented when it comes to defining love. Think back to the last movie you watched that involved some sort of romance (and since we're guys we'll stick with the movie genre "action-romance"). Of course, the hero always gets the girl. Some helpless damsel in distress gets swept off her feet by her rescuer; something inevitably blows up in the background; then the two gaze longingly into each other's eyes and passionately say, "Oh, I love you ... " Let's face it. There is a lot more to love than just adrenaline, fantasy, and short-lived emotion. Of course, it's always humorous once the sequel comes out. Later, you discover that the hero decided at some point to "move on" from his previous love interest, and has found a new girlfriend. So much for "love," I guess!

Unfortunately, our society has adopted this nebulous definition of "love." Countless times, I've heard couples announce to the world just how much they "love" each other, only for them to break up shortly thereafter. In cases like these, the concept of love is reduced down to nothing but a shallow, momentary feeling of strong affection or sexual attraction. Certainly, attraction is a valid aspect of love, but it is not all of love.

The Bible's Definition of "Love"

Now that we've taken a look at one way society defines love, let's explore what the Bible has to say about it. Fortunately, the Bible defines love a little more concretely than a mere whimsical emotion. In 1 Corinthians 13, Paul gives a solid definition of what love is and what it isn't. He defines love as:

- Being patient
- Being kind
- Rejoicing in truth
- Bearing all things
- Believing all things
- Hoping all things
- Enduring all things
- Never ending

He characterizes the opposite of love as being:

- Envious
- Boastful
- Arrogant
- Rude
- Self-seeking
- Irritable
- Resentful
- Joyful in wrongdoing

Do you notice how all of these definitions involve virtues a little deeper than just "that feeling you get when you look into each other's eyes?" I once heard a preacher define love as being an "unconditional commitment to an imperfect person."[2] This perspective revolutionized my way of thinking. Telling someone that you "love" them should be taken seriously. Love is more than just a feeling. It involves commitment.

The Ultimate Example of Love

If you are looking for a good role model for loving others, you don't have to look any further than God Himself. John 3:16 says, "For God so loved the world, that he gave his only Son, that whoever believes in him should not perish but have eternal life." Imagine how difficult it would be to lose a child. God's love for us was so great that He allowed His own Son to die on our behalf.

Let's go a step further and look at Christ's sacrificial love for us. In Philippians 2, Paul encourages us to love each other by imitating the same love that Christ showed toward us. Paul states:

> *"Have this mind among yourselves, which is yours in Christ Jesus, who, though he was in the form of God, did not count equality with God a thing to be grasped, but emptied himself, by taking the form of a servant, being born in the likeness of men. And being found in human form, he humbled himself by becoming obedient to the point of death, even death on a cross." (Philippians 2:5-8)*

Jesus loved us so much that He gave up His Godly form, became a mortal man and died a tortuous death fit only for a criminal. He once said, "Greater love has no one than this, that someone lay

[2] Holland, R. (1999, Sep. 26). *The Recognition And Reality Of A Righteous Man Part 3 by Rick Holland.* Retrieved Sep. 6, 2016, from Grace Community Church of the Valley: https://www.gracechurch.org/sermons/4994

down his life for his friends" (*John 15:13*). Christ laid down His life for us so that we could live eternal life clothed in righteousness. Now that is the ultimate example of "true love!"

Be Committed in Your Love

Hopefully, the next time you think of saying "I love you" to a girl, you will remember this chapter. Ask yourself, "Am I just saying this because my hormones are telling me to do so? Or am I actually unconditionally committing myself to this person?"

Personally, I would suggest waiting awhile before telling your significant other that you love her. "When would be the appropriate time?" you might ask? Since love involves commitment, wouldn't it make sense to wait to say "I love you" until you're actually ready to commit yourself to her? Personally, my wife and I waited until our engagement to say these words for that very reason. I'm not saying that you have to do it exactly as we did it. I am only encouraging you to take your words seriously. Don't treat the words "I love you" merely as a feeling. Rather, be committed in your love.

Start Working on Becoming Loving Now

You might ask, "What if I'm not naturally a 'loving' person?" Due to our sin nature, being loving is a struggle for everyone. It is something that has to be learned and practiced, and you can start working on this right now. Eventually, if it's God's will for you to marry, you will be charged by God to love your wife the same way Christ loves the church (*Ephesians 5*). You can practice this now by loving those around you. Jesus said, "This is my commandment, that you love one another as I have loved you" (*John 15:12*). If you work on this now, before you are married, you will find it much easier to be selfless in marriage.

True Love Until the End

When trying to think of someone I knew who strongly demonstrated love in his life, I immediately thought of my friend, Chris Drager. Let me give you a little background on him. Chris was a man who had everything going for him. He was married, adopted a child, got a seminary degree, was a brilliant biblical historian and teacher, and even became an elder at my home church. The only thing that got in his way was cancer. Chris battled this terrible illness on and off for over 10 years.

Once cancer hit him for the final time, a close friend and I knew that we didn't have much time left with him. We quickly set up a time to take him to one of his favorite local restaurants in downtown St. Paul, Minnesota. Our goal was to provide encouragement to him in the midst of his trial. But little did we know that we would be on the receiving end of encouragement that day.

When reflecting on that time, I recall Chris telling us how he had a complete peace about going home to be with the Lord, and that he was "ready." But what strikes me most even to this day is that he didn't ask for us to pray for his pain, strength, encouragement, or anything of the like. Rather, Chris asked us to pray for his wife. He knew that his passing was going to be heart-wrenching and grievous to her. Chris asked us to pray that she'd be able to find a good husband after he was gone, so she could have someone to look after her and their beloved baby girl. Chris also told us that he didn't want to pursue further cancer treatments because he didn't want to leave his wife drowning in medical debt after he was gone. His perspective stunned me. During his final, dying days he took the focus off of himself and put it on someone else. Chris sacrificially loved his wife until the very end. Are you prepared to do the same?

Chris, Emily, and Erika

Personal Reflections

1. What are some ways in which you've seen the word "love" used carelessly?

2. In your own words, describe what you think it means to truly love a woman.

3. Take a moment to reflect on Christ's sacrifice. What are some ways in which you can become more selfless in your own life?

CHAPTER 8

Marriage-Mindedness

"Let marriage be held in honor among all ... "
- Hebrews 13:4

If you were asked to define what a "romantic relationship" is, what would you say? Is it a deep emotional and physical attraction between two people? Does it involve teddy bears, roses and chocolates? The Merriam-Webster dictionary defines romance as "an emotional attraction or aura belonging to an especially heroic era, adventure, or activity."[3] You get the idea.

However you may define a romantic relationship, it is more important to define its *purpose*. Premarital relationships should not be built on flighty emotions, extravagant gifts, or starry eyes. These aspects are wonderful "bonuses," but couples shouldn't develop an interest in each other for these reasons alone. Instead, a romantic relationship should have at its foundation an intentional marriage mindset. This chapter is dedicated to helping you develop a better understanding of what being marriage-minded means.

Reasons Why People Enter Relationships

A good place to start is to look at reasons why many people enter into romantic relationships. Some seek a significant other in order to gain "status" amongst their peers. Many are driven by insecurity. Others are lonely, and have a desire for companionship. And there are some that simply want to engage sexually. Unfortunately, many of these reasons are unhealthy and blinding. As a result, these motives can lead to devastating consequences. A romantic

[3] *"romance."* Merriam-Webster.com. 2015. www.merriam-webster.com (6 Aug. 2016).

relationship should be built on something more substantial than selfish, personal gain.

"Marriage-Mindedness" is Being Intentional

Let's first ask: "What is the purpose of a premarital, romantic relationship?" As one preacher put it, the intent must be to "test the waters for marriage."[4] In other words, a relationship must adopt a *marriage-mindset*. This involves being objective about preparing for marriage practically (e.g., finances, assets) and spiritually (e.g., character, conduct). If you are in a relationship, it also involves making sure that you're on the same page with your significant other regarding convictions on issues such as faith, family, money, and mission. A relationship that is not intentional lacks direction and is dangerous. As you continue to explore the world of relationships, be sure to be intentional in your pursuits.

"Marriage-Mindedness" Involves Respecting God's Design

A significant aspect of being marriage-minded is developing a respect for God's marital institution. At the beginning of Creation, God revealed His intention for creating intimacy between male and female. Genesis 2:24 says: "For this reason a man shall leave his father and his mother, and be joined to his wife; and they shall become one flesh. *(NASB)* In addition, Jesus said in Matthew 19:6: "So they are no longer two, but one flesh. Therefore what God has joined together, let no one separate." *(NIV)* It is obvious that God designed relational intimacy to be reserved for marriage only. Since He takes marital exclusivity seriously, it's important to exercise caution while in a relationship.

---

[4] Holland, R. (1999, Sep. 5). *Eyes Wide Open by Rick Holland*. Retrieved Sep. 6, 2016, from Grace Community Church of the Valley: https://www.gracechurch.org/sermons/4991

Respect for God's marital institution is lost if a romantic relationship is void of a marriage-mindset. As husbands are commanded to "hold marriage in honor" (*Hebrews 13:4*), you (as a future husband) should also be serious about respecting marriage. Don't casually date for "fun." If you are not serious in your intentions, you are at high risk of violating boundaries that should be reserved for marriage. Handling yourself carelessly puts you at risk of hurting at least four people: the person you're interested in, that person's future spouse, your future spouse, and yourself. Marriage is about uniting one man with one woman. Don't treat it lightly.

"Marriage-Mindedness" is Not Based on a Whim

A common mistake many young people make is thinking they are being "marriage-minded" when they're actually not. For instance, it is not uncommon to hear two people say, "Oh, yes, we're planning on getting married someday," but they've stopped guarding themselves and are getting physical behind the scenes. Just "knowing in your heart" that "this is who God has for you" is not enough. Because, in reality, you don't know who your future spouse will be until you actually say, "I do." Countless times I have heard young people say, "God told me that we were meant to be in this relationship!" only for them to break up shortly afterwards. Being marriage-minded has a lot less to do with whimsical thoughts about getting married someday, and much more to do with a concerted effort to critically assess whether or not that person is the one whom God intends for you to marry.

"Marriage-Mindedness" Involves Waiting

The blessings of marriage are truly wonderful, and you will never regret waiting to enjoy them. Once in marriage, there will be plenty of opportunity to explore all of its joys. Save what is supposed to be enjoyed in marriage for the actual marriage itself.

> *"Drink water from your own cistern, flowing water from your own well. Should your springs be scattered abroad, streams of water in the streets? Let them be for yourself alone, and not for strangers with you. Let your fountain be blessed, and rejoice in the wife of your youth, a lovely deer, a graceful doe. Let her breasts fill you at all times with delight; be intoxicated always in her love." (Proverbs 5:15-19)*

Perhaps you are someone who has already "crossed the line" and experienced some of the emotional and physical aspects of a relationship that should only be reserved for marriage. No matter what point you are at, and regardless of whatever mistakes you have made, God forgives, and you can still put on a marriage-mindset starting now. It's never too late to start fresh because we know that "If we confess our sins, he is faithful and just to forgive us our sins and to cleanse us from all unrighteousness" (*1 John 1:9*).

Discovering Marriage-Mindedness

During my early teen years, I often daydreamed about the woman I would eventually marry. Since I didn't guard my heart carefully, I began to crave romance. Yes, I admit it. I'm a bit of a romantic (my wife doesn't seem to mind though).

I struggled with much insecurity in my youth. I let my life become dominated by concerns over my relationship status. "All the popular kids have girlfriends, so maybe I need one too?" "What if all the cute girls get taken, and I'd have to marry someone I'm not attracted to?"

To mask my insecurities, I convinced myself that I was being "marriage-minded" in my pursuits to find "the one." Certainly, marriage was on my mind, but that didn't mean that I was truly marriage-minded.

It wasn't until my early twenties that I came to peace about my singleness. God showed me that striving after a potential spouse was not the same thing as being marriage-minded. I then made a decision to stop pursuing relationships, and entrust to God the task of finding a spouse for me.

Ironically, God introduced my future wife to me only a few months later. (And, contrary to my childhood fears, she was gorgeous!) But because Christ had become my sufficient companion, I could pursue her differently now. Instead of jumping into a relationship in order to satisfy my insecurities, I could embrace an intentional marriage-mindset.

Personal Reflections

1. List a few examples of how someone might enter a relationship for wrong reasons.

2. Why is it important to be cautious about reserving yourself for marriage?

3. What are some ways in which you can improve upon being marriage-minded?

CHAPTER 9

The Woman to Find

"Charm is deceitful and beauty is vain,
but a woman who fears the Lord, she shall be praised."
- Proverbs 31:30 (NASB)

Often times, people create a list of desirable qualities to help them find their "perfect match." Do you have such a list? If so, what's on it? Perhaps you've included traits such as "bubbly," "beautiful," "athletic," or "funny." These lists can certainly be helpful, but it's important to use Scripture as your guide when constructing them. Otherwise, you may fall into certain traps such as expecting an imperfect human being to fit an impossible profile. Or you could get caught up with thinking that a relationship is all about your own personal fulfillment instead of refining what you have to offer. In my early twenties, I decided to discard my list. I realized that God knew me better than I knew myself, and that I couldn't trust my own judgement when it came to finding "the perfect woman."

This chapter is dedicated to helping you identify key biblical qualities to look for in a wife. More specifically, since no one is perfect, you will be encouraged to look for a woman who is *growing* or *willing to grow* in these areas. Let's now take a look at what Scripture reveals about the woman to find.

Christ Must Be Her Lord

If you have accepted Jesus Christ as your Lord and Savior, Scripture is clear that you must only marry a believer. The Apostle Paul says:

> *"Do not be unequally yoked with unbelievers. For what partnership has righteousness with lawlessness? Or what fellowship has light with*

> *darkness? What accord has Christ with [Satan]? Or what portion does a believer share with an unbeliever?" (2 Corinthians 6:14-15)*

The picture Paul uses is a "yoke." What is a "yoke?" It is not the yellow part of an egg! It is a wooden crossbar that gets harnessed to the necks of two oxen allowing them to pull a plow together. An "unequally yoked" ox team would mean that one ox is weaker than the other. Thus, the bulk of the burden rests on the strongest ox. The strong ox then becomes exhausted since the weaker ox offers no help. This illustration can be applied to relationships. You should only be interested in pursuing a believer. Otherwise, you will become weighed down by an unbelieving spouse, and struggle to be effective in your ministry to the Lord.

In addition, Paul makes it very clear that God will have nothing to do with Satan. How could you, a friend of God, unite yourself to someone who does not know the Lord, and thus is an enemy of God? If you find yourself attracted to someone who is not a Christian, you should question why you are drawn to her. How could you pursue someone who does not love your Savior? Be careful not to make the mistake of assuming that you can win her over to Christ. This is called "missionary dating," and it's a dangerous game. She may very well become a Christian at some point, but it's important to remember that only the Holy Spirit can change a person's heart.

A Submissive Spirit

Scripture teaches that wives should submit to their husbands as they depict the Church's submission to Christ.

> *"Wives, submit to your own husbands, as to the Lord. For the husband is the head of the wife even as Christ is the head of the church ... " (Ephesians 5:22-23)*

Since submissiveness is a quality that wives should possess, it's important find a woman who desires to grow in meekness and obedience.

Unfortunately, it may be difficult to tell if the woman you are interested in has this quality since she is not subject to your leadership yet. So it is a good idea to observe how well she respects the current authority figure in her life. In most cases, this would be her father. How well she treats and submits to her father will be a good indicator of how she will act toward her future husband. If their bond is strong, then that is a good sign.

A Teachable Spirit

Another character trait to look for in a woman is the same quality that you should be developing yourself: a teachable spirit. The book of Proverbs is filled with teachings such as "do not be wise in your own eyes" (*Proverbs 3:7, NASB*), and "heed instruction and be wise, and do not neglect it" (*Proverbs 8:33, NASB*). A teachable woman allows God to shape her heart through sanctification. Imagine living life with someone who is continually finding ways to improve herself for God's glory. It's a beautiful picture.

A good indicator of whether or not a girl is teachable is how well she responds to wise advice or instruction. If a teacher, church leader, friend, or family member counsels or confronts her, how does she react? Does she respond with defensiveness or unrepentant bitterness? Or is she thankful, and desires to see change occur in her life? A teachable woman is someone who actively seeks out advice from older, wiser women. Titus 2:3-5 says:

> *"Older women ... are to teach what is good, and so train the young women to love their husbands and children, to be self-controlled, pure, working at home, kind, and submissive to their own husbands, that the word of God may not be reviled."*

This kind of woman will learn what it means to become a God-honoring individual. In so-doing, she will lay the foundation for becoming a God-honoring future wife.

Guarding Her Heart

Next, it is important to look for a woman who is willing to guard her heart for her husband. Proverbs 4:23 says, "Watch over your heart with all diligence, for from it flow the springs of life" (*NASB*). Is she addicted to chick flicks and romance novels? Does she hold her heart out on a platter for men to abuse and misuse? Is she flirtatious? You have to remember, these character flaws won't magically disappear after getting married. If she does not guard her heart as a single woman, she will not be careful with how she handles herself after getting married.

It is a comfort to me knowing that the only man, besides myself, who held my wife's heart was her father. He is a tender and loving man, and I know he treasured and cared for her. What a privilege it was to have that role transferred to me, so that I could treasure her heart in the same way.

A Helping Mindset

In order to know what kind of woman to look for, it's important for you to understand the God-ordained role of your future spouse. Genesis 2:18, 22 says,

> *"Then the Lord God said, 'It is not good for the man to be alone; I will make him a <u>helper</u> suitable for him ... ' The Lord God fashioned into a woman the rib which He had taken from the man, and brought her to the man." (Emphasis added)*

God created Eve so that she could be Adam's "helper," as Eve assisted him in the garden. A wife's role is to support her husband in the ministries and responsibilities that God has set before him. Furthermore, Scripture indicates that wives should develop a helping mindset toward their families in the home. Titus 2:4a-5 says:

> *" ... Encourage the young women to love their husbands, to love their children, to be sensible, pure, workers at home, kind, being subject to their own husbands, so that the word of God will not be dishonored." (Emphasis added, NASB)*

Based on these passages, it's important to look for a woman who has a heart for tending to familial needs. Ask these questions:

"Does she have a heart of service for her family?"

"Is she patient and loving toward children?"

"Does she look for ways to serve God in her church and community?"

Observe how she interacts with others. This will help you discern whether or not she has a helping mindset.

Self-Control

As mentioned earlier, in Titus 2 Paul encourages the "older women ... to train the young women ... to be self-controlled." Self-control is a virtue that can be applied to many areas of life (entertainment, eating, habits, etc.). This will particularly be important when it comes to finances. I know one non-Christian who almost divorced his wife because she secretly accrued tens-of-thousands of dollars of credit card debt. A woman who has no control over her spending will bring major financial stress to the marriage.

If you are currently interested in a girl, take a moment to assess how she handles her money. Don't let her habit of "spontaneous spending" somehow become "cute." Later on, it certainly won't be "cute" if she frivolously spends the hard-earned money intended for your family's needs.

Instead of an uncontrolled spender, look for someone who is willing to learn how to save and give. As Jesus said, " ... 'It is more blessed to give than to receive'" (*Acts 20:35*). Giving reveals a self-sacrificial heart, and marriage involves sacrificing oneself for another

Modesty

Let's talk about modesty. Just as you should strive to be pure for your future wife, a woman should do her best to reserve her beauty for her future husband. 1 Timothy 2:9 says, "I also want the women to dress modestly, with decency and propriety ... " (*NIV*). If you are interested in someone, how does she dress? Does she wear clothes that are tight-fitting or revealing? Modesty should be a priority in her life.

Now, a girl is not responsible for the minds of the men around her, but she certainly should be doing her best to not cause them to stumble. An immodest woman reveals a lack of love for her future husband. Instead of saving her body for her husband, she flaunts it around for the sinful enjoyment of others. A woman striving after purity can always find modest clothing. Might there be a chance that she will have to sacrifice on "style" a little? Maybe. But being pure and modest is much more important than looking "trendy."

A Proverbs 31 Woman or Proverbs 7 Adulteress?

Let's take a moment to compare two different examples of women in the book of Proverbs. First, let's look at Proverbs 7. This chapter gives a very vivid picture of a man "lacking sense" who wanders near the house of a woman known to be "boisterous and rebellious." Her character is described as having "feet [that] do not remain at home." She is one who "dresses as a prostitute, wily of heart." She seduces the man to come into her house while her husband is away on a trip. Scripture describes this man as an "ox [that] goes to the slaughter." Ultimately, this story ends in the devastating death of this man's soul and body.

Learn from this man's story. Don't repeat his mistake. The writer encourages you to "not let your heart turn aside to her ways [...] her house is the way to [Hell], going down to the chambers of death." Avoid this kind of immoral woman at all costs. Your spiritual and physical wellbeing are at stake.

In contrast, let's take a look at a Proverbs 31 woman. Proverbs 31:10-11 says, "An excellent wife who can find? She is far more precious than jewels. The heart of her husband trusts in her, and he will have no lack of gain." Proverbs describes this "jewel" as being trustworthy. She is a woman characterized by doing "good and not evil." This is someone who is productive "[looking] well to the ways of her household, and does not eat the bread of idleness." She is also someone who is skilled or educated. "She makes linen garments and sells them, and supplies belts to the tradesmen." She is also wise and kind. "She opens her mouth in wisdom, and the teaching of kindness is on her tongue."

Doesn't she sound amazing? Her family thinks so too. "Her children rise up and call her blessed; her husband also, and he praises her: 'Many women have done excellently, but you surpass them all.'"

What a contrast between these two women! You've probably heard the following verse a thousand times, but hopefully you now have a deeper understanding of its meaning. Proverbs 31:30 says, "Charm is deceitful and beauty is vain, but a woman who fears the Lord, she shall be praised" (*NASB*). There is a radical difference between the

Proverbs 7 woman and the Proverbs 31 woman. Look for a woman who strives to honor God in every area of her life.

Concluding Thoughts

This chapter is not intended to be an exhaustive list of all the qualities that a woman should possess. It's also not meant to imply that you can only marry someone who lives out these principles in complete perfection. Certainly, no one is perfect. But this chapter is meant to help train your mind to look for someone who has a desire to grow all areas of her life for God's glory.

You will find that there are not many women today who take these values seriously, but be encouraged. If it is God's will for you to marry, He knows who your future spouse is, and will reveal her to you in His perfect timing. With this in mind, start praying for the well-being of your future spouse. Pray that God would convict her to grow in these areas. You never know, she may be praying for you right now.

A Woman Worth Pursuing

I remember a conversation I had with a friend in college. He asked me why I was still single, so I gave him my backstory. He then asked me, "Why not just find someone you find attractive and start dating her? You don't have to be interested in someone who's religious. You both could just come to a mutual agreement and respect each other's views." I responded, "Actually, I will only marry a Christian. My first love is Christ. She would have to love Him just as much as, or more than I do for me to even be interested." He seemed astounded by my answer, and proceeded to tell me that he'd never heard someone say something like that before.

A woman who goes beyond her own spiritual walk and assists you to maintain a pure mindset is quite rare. I've been blessed with this type of rare jewel. During our engagement, my wife helped to remind me of a striking reality whenever I was tempted to push physical boundaries. She would say, "Remember, Michael, waiting for marriage means that you are only saving me for yourself. Why not wait for God's proper timing?" This reminder fought directly against my physical desires, but constructively fed my spiritual needs. We, as men, are ultimately responsible for maintaining a pure mindset. But a woman who unwaveringly speaks truth into your life is a woman worth pursuing.

Mandy

Personal Reflections

1. Why is it important to only pursue a Christian?

2. What are some traits of a Proverbs 7 woman, and why is it important to avoid this type of person?

3. What traits do you value in a woman, and how do they compare to the Biblical characteristics listed in this chapter?

CHAPTER 10

Initiating a Relationship

*"He who finds a wife finds a good thing
and obtains favor from the Lord."
- Proverbs 18:22*

Have you ever thought, "How will I know 'the one' when I meet her?" Perhaps you've already identified a girl, and are wondering how to go about expressing your feelings to her. The intent of this chapter is to help you develop a biblical frame of mind during these early, and sometimes delicate, stages. Instead of feeling perplexed by the subject of initiating a relationship, my hope is that you will gain a greater sense of peace and confidence in this area.

Meeting Her on God's Timing and His Terms

The wait leading up to meeting "the one" can sometimes be wearisome. It's easy to let your mind be plagued with questions such as: When will I meet her? Where will I meet her? How will I know if she's the right one? Perhaps you've already imagined some scenarios as to how it might happen. As you turn a corner at school, you accidentally bump into a random girl causing her to drop her belongings. You scramble to your knees to help recover the scattered items. You take a moment to look up only to have your eyes meet hers. At that moment, you realize something profound: "She's the one!"

Or, maybe, you're more of the "heroic" type. You've got it all planned out perfectly in your mind. An attractive girl you know from school starts walking across a busy street. You immediately notice that there's a vehicle headed straight for her. Courageously, you dash toward her, push her out of harm's way, and incur the blow. Of course, you only receive minor injuries, and she immediately becomes enamored by your valiant actions (not to mention, good looks).

As humorous as these scenarios are, I think most of us would be lying if we said we never had thoughts like this cross our minds. But, to be quite honest, when or how you meet your future wife really shouldn't consume your thought life. The fact is that you don't know the timing or circumstances under which God will introduce you to her. But what you can take comfort in, is that He has a plan set in place for you. He may bring you and your soulmate together in a way that you never expected. Proverbs 16:9 says, "The heart of man plans his way, but the Lord establishes his steps." Since God holds your future in His hands, let Him work out the details of your love story.

Next, take a moment to ponder the following passage:

> *"The steadfast love of the Lord never ceases; his mercies never come to an end; they are new every morning; great is your faithfulness. 'The Lord is my portion,' says my soul, 'therefore I will hope in him.' The Lord is good to those who wait for him, to the soul who seeks him. It is good that one should wait quietly for the salvation of the Lord." (Lamentations 3:22-26)*

This passage is packed with truth that can assist you as you wait for your future spouse. It speaks of the assurance of God's love and faithfulness, and emphasizes the satisfaction that can be found in Him. The writer also depicts the beauty of those who wait quietly on God's timing as they seek Him. Isn't this passage so rich? As you longingly wait for a spouse, remember God's faithfulness and love for you. He will surely bless those who patiently wait on Him.

Observe and Look for Proven Character

If you find yourself interested in a girl, take time to observe the maturity of her character. Begin asking questions that will help you assess whether or not she has *proven* character. What patterns exist in her in her life? What do her actions say about her? How does she interact with others? Is she a new believer? Does she look to apply God's Word to her life?

In Matthew 13, Jesus taught a parable about a sower who planted seed in the field. The seed (God's Word) fell in various types of soil (people's hearts): hard, rocky, thorny, and fertile. The hard ground represents the hearts of people who reject God's Word immediately. The rocky and thorny soils depict people who are at first excited about following God, but eventually turn their backs on Him because of hardship and worldly lusts. Finally, the good soil represents hearts that allow God's Word to "take root" in their lives, allowing their faith to endure and thrive.

It's good to reflect on this passage if you are thinking about pursuing a woman. Don't rush. Rather, be patient and observe the general trajectory of her life to understand which "soil" she belongs to. If she is young, it may be a good idea to wait to see what happens to her character as she transitions out of adolescence into adulthood. Many times, a person's true character becomes exposed upon reaching independence. If she is in high school, maybe allow for some time to pass to see how well she withstands the pressures and temptations that young adults commonly face. Be wise by making an effort to gain a fuller understanding of a woman's character before gaining too much momentum.

A Peace About Pursuing Through Prayer

So what should you do if you think you've met *her*? How do you know if it's the right time to pursue? Once you start asking questions like these, the first thing to do is *pray*! As stated in an earlier chapter, Philippians 4:6-7 says:

> *"... be not anxious about anything, but in everything by prayer and supplication with thanksgiving let your requests be made known to God. And the peace of God, which surpasses all understanding, will guard your hearts and your minds in Christ Jesus."*

After making a pure-hearted request for God's guidance, look for a "peace that surpasses all understanding." If you obtain this peace, you can rest in God's blessing upon that direction. If you don't have peace, God may be trying to bring something to your attention. The girl you're interested in may not be your destined spouse. Or perhaps your heart requires evaluation. Or God may simply desire for you to wait on His timing. Be very sensitive to move in step with the Holy Spirit's leading through prayer, and He will guide you to the right woman.

Get Counsel

If you begin taking an interest in a woman, and are wondering if it's a good idea to initiate a relationship, consider getting counsel! Get the opinion of wise men and women on whether or not you're "ready" for a relationship. Tell them about your financial, educational, and spiritual state to get their perspective. If they personally know the girl that you're interested in, ask them what they think about her! Proverbs 15:22 says, "Without counsel plans fail, but with many advisers they succeed." There is success in an abundance of wise counsel. Don't wait to get it until it's too late.

Clarity of Intentions

If you are single, you may be wondering how to actually initiate a relationship with a girl you're interested in. Well, if you've gained a peace about pursuing her through counsel and prayer, then it's quite simple. Tell her that you're interested! Convey to her that you would like to get to know her better to see if she is the one God intends for you to marry. In other words, *be clear about your intentions*. It's that simple. Don't make it more complicated than what it needs to be if it's in your power to do so.

Unfortunately, many couples enter "pseudo-relationships" where they haven't made a clear commitment to a serious relationship. This can cause a lot of heartache and drama. For example, stress, jealousy, and confusion may occur over "who likes who;" and concerns may arise when she starts talking to other guys. Be the one who establishes a mutual understanding of your intentions. Ideally, it would be best to do this at the beginning. Might she turn you down? Maybe. Will she tell you to go talk to her Dad first? That's what happened to me! The fact is, if God has given you a "peace that passes all understanding," then why not do something about it?

Guard Your Heart While Getting to Know Her

Leading up to, and during the early stages of a relationship, it's important to guard your heart from getting attached too quickly. What if the girl you are interested in doesn't share mutual feelings? Or what if one or both of you discover that this relationship "wasn't meant to be" after a few weeks of getting to know each other? If you become too attached, it may be hard to let go. And if you can't let go, you strive against God's will. Psalm 46:10 says, "Cease striving, and know that I am God ... " (*NASB*). As exciting as it is to initiate a relationship, be sober throughout the process. Allow the relationship to progress naturally according to God's will, and, if it's meant to be, you'll experience a God-given peace.

Respect Her Parents

Finally, if the woman you're interested in has parents present in her life, it is good to show them respect. She is commanded to "honor [her] father and mother" (*Exodus 20:12*), and you must do what you can to encourage her in this area. One way you can show respect for her parents' authority is to ask for her father's permission to pursue her when initiating the relationship. As old fashioned as this may seem, it sets a tone of respect that will help both you and her honor God.

Concluding Thoughts

Hopefully, you feel more equipped on the topic of initiating a relationship after having read this chapter. Even if you are already in a relationship, many of the principles mentioned are still applicable to you. In your pursuits, trust God, observe character, acquire peace through prayer, get counsel, have clarity of intentions, guard your heart, and respect parental authority. In doing so, God will bless your endeavors to honor Him.

How It All Started

At this point, you might be curious about how "it all started" for me and my wife Mandy. So I thought that I'd share my personal story of how God initiated our relationship in a way I could never have predicted.

During my junior year of high school, I received an invitation to perform in a Christmas concert at a church near Stillwater, Minnesota. I performed an arrangement of "What Child Is This?" on the classical guitar. After the performance, I was introduced to one of the other musicians who happened to be a flutist. Her name was Mandy Potts (you should try saying her name with a British accent—it's fun!). She was a blonde-haired, green-eyed beauty. Beyond her looks, there was something very different about her. Unlike many girls, she was neither flirtatious, cold, nor indifferent. She radiated genuine kindness while maintaining a balanced and guarded nature. I was struck with how odd it felt to have a natural, uncomplicated conversation with someone of the opposite sex. Even though our conversation was brief, that moment will be forever burned in my mind.

Unintentionally, our paths crossed at various events such as bonfires, orchestral performances, and graduation parties. However, our contact gradually dissipated upon completing high school.

A few years later, I left home to work as an intern at an engineering company in Wisconsin. My family teased me by saying that I would inevitably meet my future wife during that summer. Somewhat stubbornly, I became determined to prove them wrong. I was set on guarding my heart, and nothing was going to change that. At least, so I thought.

While devoting myself to ministry and fellowship at my Wisconsin church, I received an unexpected web message from a girl I hadn't seen or talked to for years. It was Mandy Potts! I had to reel back my excitement, and remind myself to stay guarded. I sent a casual message back, and thought nothing would ever come of it. She sent an apologetic reply informing me that she had contacted me by mistake. But our conversations only continued, and her depth of character and love for God became evident.

Eventually, I came to the realization that God was at work! Our conversations seemed so natural, and I was starting to become interested in her. I prayed, "Lord, she seems like she's a strong believer. You've brought this situation to me. Is this a direction you want me to pursue?" I decided to not strive, but rather let God do the leading.

I asked for her phone number to get to know her better. Our phone conversations continued throughout the remainder of my internship.

Just before I moved back to Minnesota, I knew that our friendship was turning into something much more. She displayed characteristics that I found attractive for a future spouse. So I decided to talk about it with my father and pastor to get their insight, and I asked God for wisdom.

On my drive back home to Minnesota, I called Mandy. I told her that I was interested in her, and that she seemed like the type of woman I'd like to marry someday. But, to my surprise, her only response was, "That's very kind of you, but if you're interested in me, you'll have to talk to my Dad first." I thought, "Well, she didn't say 'no!' So, I suppose that's a good sign!" But, in all seriousness, I was astounded by how much peace I felt about her response. She demonstrated a respect for her father, and this gave me confidence in her character. I called her father the next day, and we set up a time to meet.

Three days later, I nervously waited at the doorstep of a Mexican restaurant where I planned to meet Mandy's father. All that I knew about him was that he used to be a rugged mountain man, owned a red truck, and was very protective of his daughter. I thought, "This guy is going to grill me."

Eventually, I saw a little truck drive into the parking lot. Out stepped a man who was about four-to-five inches shorter than me. He walked calmly toward me in his leather cowboy boots. He had a gentle smile on his face, a warm demeanor, and gave me a friendly greeting, requesting that I call him "Walt." He invited me into the restaurant and insisted that he pay for our meal. He was a humble man who seemed to have had experienced much in his lifetime. It became evident that his life's only goal was to bring glory to His

Creator. All the "rough" questions I thought he was going to ask me were never brought up. Instead, he just asked me about my career goals, whether or not I was a believer, what church I attended, and explained to me just how special "Amanda" was to him. This was not the kind of interaction that I expected to have! To say the least, I was relieved. Little did I know, at the time, that this man would eventually become not just my father-in-law, but a close friend and wise mentor.

A few days later, Walt invited me to spend time at Mandy's grandparents' lake house in order to give me an opportunity to get to know her and the family better. Talk about pressure! I hadn't even seen Mandy in person for several years, and I was going to meet her and her entire family all at once! Of course, I accepted gladly.

I still remember our first interaction as if it were yesterday. I drove up to the lakefront home and took the time to pray and calm my nerves. Mandy's family was running late, but a few minutes later, I saw the same little red truck driving in my direction. The truck parked next to my car, and Walt stepped out to greet me. While speaking to him, I could see in the corner of my eye the blonde-haired, green-eyed beauty getting out of the vehicle. I took a deep breath, and looked in her direction. That's when our eyes met. With a big smile, she came and greeted me with a hug. The rest of the day was filled with the joy of getting to know Mandy and her family.

After that day, God provided me with a peace about pursuing her. I then asked her out on a tea date, and our relationship never lost momentum.

It's quite humorous looking back at the irony of our story. How we got to know each other might seem to be quite unconventional. But, of course, God was in every detail. He brought peace and allowed everything to progress naturally. Praise God for His perfect plan.

"But seek first the kingdom of God and his righteousness, and all these things will be added to you."
- Matthew 6:33

Personal Reflections

1. Are you currently interested in a girl? If so, what actions have you taken to come to a peace about pursuing her?

2. If you're currently interacting with a girl for romantic reasons, in what ways have you made it clear that you are marriage-minded?

3. How can you improve upon the way you're going about waiting for or pursuing a woman?

CHAPTER 11

Conduct in a Relationship

"So I do not run aimlessly; I do not box as one beating the air. But I discipline my body and keep it under control, lest ... I myself should be disqualified."
- 1 Corinthians 9:26-27

Up to this point, we've looked at topics involving salvation, character, contentment, purity, practical responsibility, biblical love, and how to help your fellow sisters. We've also learned how to apply biblical principles concerning marriage-mindedness, qualities to look for in a woman, and initiating a relationship. As we transition into the subject of conduct in a relationship, it's important to remember that all of the previous principles are still pertinent. With this in mind, let's narrow our focus. Let's take a close look at how we, as men, should go about conducting ourselves while in a relationship.

What the Bible Has to Say About the Relationship "Process"

Have you ever wondered, "What does the Bible have to say about the *process* to follow in order to get married?" Certainly, Scripture lists examples of how couples came together, but the processes might surprise you as being somewhat impractical.

For example, Naomi encouraged her daughter-in-law, Ruth, to pursue Boaz. She told Ruth to wait until he was asleep " ... then go and uncover his feet and lie down, and he will tell you what to do" (*Ruth 3:3-4*). If I am ever blessed with a daughter someday, I guarantee you that I will *not* be giving her this kind of instruction!

What about Isaac and Rebekah's story? Isaac's father, Abraham, asked a servant to go find a distant relative to marry Isaac. The servant traveled and pleaded with the Lord for a sign. The servant prayed:

> *"Let the young woman to whom I shall say, 'Please let down your jar that I may drink,' and who shall say, 'Drink, and I will water your camels'—let her be the one whom you have appointed for your servant Isaac." (Genesis 24:14)*

How would you like to be in Isaac's situation? Imagine your father asking a friend to choose a woman you've never met to become your bride!

Neither of these "biblical relationship processes" would be considered ideal by today's standards. And as you read more examples from Scripture, you will find that there is not one clearly laid-out formula.

A Greater Emphasis on the Person and Not the Process

If you were hoping to find "5 Easy Steps to Pursuing a Woman for Marriage," then you will be quite disappointed. The fact is that there isn't a perfect formula. Your story may look very different from others'. But let me provide you with some encouragement. While it's true that the Bible may not have an exact process laid out for pre-marital romantic relationships, it has plenty to say about conduct, character, and general relationships. Naturally, skills learned in these areas will overlap with pre-martial and marital relationships. Your focus should be on refining your own heart and assessing hers, rather than fine-tuning a perfect process.

Unfortunately, many people in Christian circles mistakenly assume that a successful marriage is a direct result of the process taken to get there. Certainly, sinful beginnings can bring about damaging consequences, but I am speaking more about the relationship formulas in which many Christians place their trust. Terms such as "dating" and "courting" are commonly thrown around. But, interestingly, no one can really seem to agree on what those terms truly mean or look like. Is a "date" spending time one-on-one at a coffee shop with the intentions of "testing the waters" for marriage? Or is "dating" jumping frivolously from girl-to-girl just for the "fun of it"?

I have known many well-intentioned people who've claimed to have discovered the "biblical model" for relationships. Sometimes this might involve following a rigid set of rules. For example, engaging in group settings only, never spending time alone with each other, and similar rules suddenly become "God's way." Some people become so caught up in the process itself that they completely overlook major personal character flaws. Even if marriage is the result, their sin won't magically disappear. Following a rigid set of rules will not produce a successful relationship, but, by God's strength, two people with right hearts can.

God made it clear to the Israelites that He is more concerned with hearts than with processes. He said, "For I desire steadfast love and not sacrifice, the knowledge of God rather than burnt offerings" (*Hosea 6:6*). Since God is more concerned about hearts, shouldn't you be as well? Place a greater emphasis on developing your own character and assessing the heart of the woman you're interested in, rather than getting too caught up in a process.

Respecting Each Other's Convictions

After initiating a relationship, it is wise to have a conversation with your significant other to understand each other's convictions. Once you have done so, commit to respecting those boundaries. This is critical because 1 Corinthians 8 speaks of the importance of not causing a fellow brother (or, in this case, sister) to sin against his (or her) conscience.

While my wife and I were engaged, Mandy's conscience convicted her to reserve kissing for marriage. At the time, I was okay with kissing during our engagement, but I decided to respect her decision. It would have been wrong of me to pressure Mandy to kiss before our wedding. If I pushed her to sin against her conscience before marriage, what confidence could she have in my ability to lead her in purity as a husband? Clearly defining boundaries can really help to keep your significant other from stumbling. Be a true leader, and assist her in maintaining a pure conscience.

Putting Up Appropriate Safeguards

As part of God's design for our bodies, we have natural desires that respond to things such as physical closeness, kissing, etc. These actions push us closer toward consummating the relationship, which is, of course, an act that God desires to be strictly reserved for marriage. With this in mind, it's good to avoid anything that might influence you to violate God's design. For some, physical touch will cause temptation. For others, time spent alone might be too much to handle. It's extremely important to honestly assess what situations, actions, etc., might cause you to experience temptation. As Romans 13:13-14 says: "Let us walk properly ... not in sexual immorality ... But put on the Lord Jesus Christ, and make no provision for the flesh, to gratify its desires."

Be serious about making no provisions to sin. Ultimately, you will have to be wise enough to recognize what boundaries are necessary, and be disciplined enough to restrain yourself.

It's also good to have a healthy sense of distrust in how you will respond to a given situation. Sure, when you're chatting with your buddies about your "standards", it's easy to say something like, "Oh, I'd never do [fill in the blank]!" But, once you're in the moment sitting alone next to an extremely attractive female, you might just have second thoughts about your so-called "convictions." As 1

Corinthians 10:12 says, "Therefore let anyone who thinks that he stands take heed lest he fall."

Once, during our engagement, Mandy's family kindly offered a place for me to spend the night. At the time, I worked out-of-state and was coming home for the weekend to visit my fiancée for Valentine's Day (just five months before our wedding). The problem was that Mandy's family would not be home the night that I would be in town. It would be just the two of us, spending the night in the same house alone. Hopefully, at this point, you recognize the precariousness of the situation! In the end, Mandy and I decided that I should spend the night at a friend's house instead. Even though we couldn't foresee ourselves making any serious mistakes, we realized that the circumstance called for special precautions.

Get Outside Opinions

Next, do what I've encouraged you to do before. That is, get counsel! Get outside opinions from other sources besides your own or your circle of peers. Get them from mature family members, friends, and church leaders. Expose your relationship to as many wise people as possible, and get their input as to what they think. They may see something that you don't, and may be able to provide valuable insight. If you truly want to determine if your significant other is right for you, wouldn't you want to gain as much input as possible?

Honoring Her Parents

Let's assume for a moment that your significant other is still under her parents' authority, and that they are walking closely with God. Similar to the last chapter, she has been charged to "obey [her] parents in everything" according to Colossians 3:20. Since she is called to obedience, respect her parents' authority over her until she is handed over to you at the marriage altar.

In the case that her parents are not believers, this situation becomes much more difficult to address. Perhaps they deny you permission to marry their daughter because of your faith. In these types of situations, it is best to make a case-by-case assessment. I suggest that you get counsel from wise Christians (such as your pastor) to help guide you through such a hardship. Through it all, it will still be necessary to show her parents the same love and respect that you would show to anyone else. Be in prayer, and do your best not to "burn bridges."

A Momentum Toward Marriage

In previous chapters, we discussed the importance of marriage-mindedness when initiating a relationship. After doing so, you must also maintain a momentum that drives your relationship towards marriage. In other words, you should diligently test God's will to see if you are pursuing the right woman.

Unfortunately, many couples end up in stagnant relationships, and lose sight of the purpose of their relationship. Instead of working toward their future marriage, they seem content with being simply "boyfriend and girlfriend." This mentality lacks marriage-mindedness, and, over long periods of time, can produce temptation.

Be Cautious About Assuming That She's the "One"

As exciting as relationships are, it's important to exercise caution when assuming that you'll one day marry your significant other. James 4:13-15 emphasizes the fact that we do not know what the future holds:

> *"Come now, you who say, 'Today or tomorrow we will go into such and such a town and spend a year there and trade and make a profit'— yet you do*

> *not know what tomorrow will bring ... Instead you ought to say, "If the Lord wills, we will live and do this or that."*

Often times, young men assume too early that they will one day marry the one that they're dating. As a result, they become too comfortable in their interactions. Due to unforeseen circumstances, the relationship ends, leaving a trail of regret over things that were said and done. Years later, after truly finding the "one," they struggle when having to face their significant other's simple question: "Did you ever [fill in the blank] a girl before?" Because girls often value "firsts" (first kiss, first time holding hands, first time saying "I love you," etc.) the answer to that question may cause heartache. Even though you can't change the past and are forgiven in God's eyes, it's important to be wise about how you handle yourself going forward.

You won't know for sure who the "one" is until you say "I do" at the marriage altar. So until you're married, respect the fact that she could very well be someone else's future spouse. When engaging with someone of the opposite sex, ask yourself, "If my future spouse was with me right now, would she be okay with how I'm behaving toward this person?"

Concluding Thoughts

Now that you've read this chapter, I hope you feel better prepared for how you will conduct yourself in a relationship. Remember to place a greater emphasis on personal character than on a process. Gain clarity of convictions, and commit to respecting them. Do your best to put up appropriate safeguards to reduce temptation. Honor her parents. Get counsel. Be marriage-minded. And, finally, be cautious about assuming that she's the "one" until you say "I do."

How We Approached Our Relationship

Perhaps you're wondering how my wife and I went about getting to know each other before marriage. In this case, I thought I would share our example. It's important to note that our approach to our relationship should not be considered the "ideal model." It is just one way that a couple can get to know each other. Ultimately, you must follow the Lord's leading in your own convictions.

When I was first getting to know Mandy, I chose to spend time with her in both public and private settings. I figured that I would get a fuller understanding of who she was if I got to know her in a variety of circumstances.

We spent a lot of time together around family, friends and our churches. These situations allowed us to observe how each person interacted with others in a variety of different circumstances. As a result, I was able to ask questions such as: How does she serve those who are in need? Does she treat her family with respect? Does she genuinely care for friends? How strong is her faith?

Even though we had to make occasional adjustments to reduce temptation, we also enjoyed a lot of one-on-one time as a couple. Some of our most meaningful interactions took place during Friday morning tea dates at her college's coffee shop. Through dinner dates, carriage rides, and more, we had great opportunities to get to know each other's personalities, convictions, and character without much interruption.

By the time we got married, we had a very good idea as to who the other person was. We felt at peace knowing that we did our best to honor God in our endeavors.

Personal Reflections

1. Why is it more important to focus on assessing personal character rather than fine-tuning a perfect relationship process?

2. Why is it important to respect the convictions of the girl you're interested in?

3. If you are currently in a relationship, what improvements can you make to your conduct?

CHAPTER 12

Your Future Role

"Women were created from the rib of the man to be beside him; not from his head to top him, nor from his feet to be trampled by him, but from under his arm to be protected by him, near his heart to be loved by him."
- Matthew Henry

Even if you are years away from getting married, it's not too soon to start refining qualities that will prove vital in marriage. Saying "I do" doesn't magically change you into a better person. The man you are before your wedding is the man you will be afterwards. Since your character won't change overnight, you must begin preparing for marriage now.

In this chapter, we'll explore the biblical qualities of a righteous husband. This study is by no means intended to present an exhaustive list of all the traits that a husband should possess. Instead, it is meant to give you a starting point to help you understand some of God's requirements for husbands. In doing so, my hope is that you will be encouraged to start preparing for your future role.

God's Design for Marriage

In order to discover how you, as a future husband, should operate in marriage, it is key to understand God's original intent for marital roles. The best place to start your search is to look all the way back to the very beginning of creation. The book of Genesis shows that God created the heavens, earth, sky, land, stars, heavenly bodies, aquatic life, and land-dwelling creatures. After doing so, God declared it all to be "good."

Then God created a man, named "Adam," who was made in God's image. But God says something interesting at this point. For the first time, He declared that something was "not good." He said, " ... 'It is not good for the man to be alone; I will make him a helper suitable for him'" (*Genesis 2:18, NASB*). Adam was incomplete by himself. He was missing something vital. So God brought to Adam all the birds and beasts to show him that nothing that God had created up to that point would complete him. What happened next was utterly profound:

> *"So the Lord God caused a deep sleep to fall upon the man, and while he slept took one of his ribs and closed up its place with flesh. And the rib that the Lord God had taken from the man he made into a woman and brought her to the man. Then the man said, 'This at last is bone of my bones and flesh of my flesh; she shall be called Woman, because she was taken out of Man.' Therefore a man shall leave his father and his mother and hold fast to his wife, and they shall become one flesh." (Genesis 2:21-24)*

How fascinating! It is clear that God's intention was to show that man was incomplete without woman. Even Adam recognized this fact. You can sense the sound of desperation and satisfaction in his voice when he cried "at last!" God created Eve so that she could become Adam's "suitable helper" as he tended to the Garden of Eden.

Your Future Role as a Leader

Now that you better understand God's intention for creating male and female, let's take a moment to acknowledge your future leadership role as a husband. Ephesians 5:22-24 says:

> *"Wives, submit to your own husbands, as to the Lord. For the husband is the head of the wife even*

> *as Christ is the head of the church, his body, and is himself its Savior. Now as the church submits to Christ, so also wives should submit in everything to their husbands."*

In addition, 1 Peter 3:1, 5 says:

> *"Likewise, wives, be subject to your own husbands ... For this is how the holy women who hoped in God used to adorn themselves, by submitting to their own husbands ... "*

These passages reveal that God intends for you, a future husband, to lead your wife in marriage. Before you get a big head on your shoulders, you should understand that being a leader of a family is a huge undertaking that should not be taken lightly. You will answer to God for how well you guide your family. Take this seriously. *Now* is the time to start learning how to become an effective leader.

Understanding a Wife's Vulnerable Position

Being the "leader" in the relationship requires much caution and understanding. 1 Peter 3:7 says:

> *"You husbands in the same way, live with your wives in an understanding way, as with someone weaker, since she is a woman; and show her honor as a fellow heir of the grace of life, so that your prayers will not be hindered." (NASB)*

Your wife will be placed in a precarious and vulnerable position. She is commanded to subject herself to an imperfect person (you). You, as the man, have to answer to a perfect Person (God). You can put your full faith in Him to do the right thing. On the other hand, a woman has to submit herself to someone she knows will do things wrong at some point. That can be quite scary for her, and it's imperative that you live with her with this understanding. Your headship is not a privilege to be abused.

For now, start practicing sensitivity in your conduct toward others. Don't trample on people when it comes time to make a decision. Practice maintaining a steady, kind, considerate and loving leadership to those around you. This will help sharpen your character in preparation for your future role.

God's Command for a Man to Selflessly Love His Wife

It is absolutely necessary to understand that marriage is a reflection of Christ's relationship with His church. You will be required to act toward your future wife with the same love that Christ shows toward you. Let's take a look at what Paul has to say in Ephesians 5:

> *"Husbands, love your wives, as Christ loved the church and gave himself up for her, that he might sanctify her, having cleansed her by the washing of water with the word, so that he might present the church to himself in splendor, without spot or wrinkle or any such thing, that she might be holy and without blemish" (Ephesians 5:25-27).*

Paul encourages husbands to love their wives as Christ loves the church. How much did Christ love His children? So much so that He suffered and died on a cross for them. This models the level of dedication and love that you should be willing to show toward your future wife. Paul continues on to say:

> *"In the same way husbands should love their wives as their own bodies. He who loves his wife loves himself. For no one ever hated his own flesh, but nourishes and cherishes it, just as Christ does the church, because we are members of his body" (Ephesians 5:28-30).*

Since you are to cherish your wife in the same way that Christ loves you, it is clear that there is no room for selfishness in marriage. You will have to put aside your own wants and desires in order to attend to your wife's needs. With this in mind, start working on developing a self-sacrificial nature. Practice selfless love toward others around you. The one you will choose to love will be the one you are required to love. It is much better to learn selfless love now, rather than wait and painfully sort it out in marriage.

Conclusion

I hope this preview of marriage has helped you better understand what God requires of husbands. Since you will eventually be charged to lovingly lead your wife, it is wise to start applying these principles to your daily life now. Be serious about refining your character now, and in doing so, you will be better equipped to become an effective future husband.

A Lesson on Selfless Love

Shortly after I expressed an interest in pursuing Mandy, she told me that we needed to talk about something serious. She said, "What I'm about to tell you could potentially change your mind about our relationship, and if you choose to walk away I won't hold it against you." She paused for a moment then continued to say, "Michael, I am so thankful for your interest in me, but I have to let you know about my physical condition. For several years, I've been battling a chronic illness which affects my daily strength and stamina." She went on to explain how she got it, how it affects her now, and what life would be like going forward.

At first, I had no issue with it. In fact, I even liked the idea of being her "knight in shining armor." The thought of having someone dependent upon me appealed to my sense of "selfless heroism."

But as time went on, the illness began to put a slight strain on our relationship. I still remember having to cancel our first movie date because her energy was low. You would think that my natural response would be filled with graciousness and understanding. But instead, I felt upset by the inconvenience. I thought to myself, "How come we can't go to a theater? Why can't watching a movie be restful?" My reaction to this situation was only a small window into the selfishness that resided in my heart.

Eventually, our wedding day came and went. We enjoyed the bliss and excitement of new marriage for a few months. But as time went on, the illness began to weigh on our marriage. Additionally, Mandy began battling a bad leg infection which would last for half a year. My fast-paced, undisciplined, bachelor lifestyle quickly proved to be incompatible with her health and stamina. Physical recreational activities had to be dismissed, time spent with friends had to be limited, late nights were spent at hospitals, and medication began interfering with our communication. I suddenly woke up to the realization of how my life had changed. My desires to fulfill my own wants began conflicting with the clear message that I must serve my wife.

Bitterness began developing inside me. During a particularly difficult night, I asked God, "Lord, why does this have to happen to me? I thought marriage was going to be different!"

That night, I wrestled with God as Jacob did in the Book of Genesis. I did not want to let go of my selfishness. I struggled with the realization that I would have to completely let go of my own wants in order to meet my wife's needs. But God convicted me with the words of Ephesians 5:25: "Husbands, love your wives, as Christ loved the church and gave himself up for her." I realized that Christ loved His Church so much that He gave up *everything* for her. Not only did He give up His very God-nature to become a lowly human (*Philippians 2:5-8*), but He also suffered and died a death fit only for a criminal on my behalf. These passages made me realize that I had to empty myself of all selfishness, and embrace the privilege of loving my wife as Christ loves me. If God sacrificed so much for me, how could I not afford to give up just a little for Mandy?

God introduced these circumstances into my life for obvious reasons. Because He loves me, He is showing me that there is no room for selfishness in marriage, and that much joy can be found in giving oneself up for another.

My journey of discovering selflessness has only begun, and I have a long way to go. But as each day goes by, I gain a deeper appreciation for the depth and beauty of the vows I made to my darling wife on our wedding day:

I, Michael, take you, Mandy,
to be my lawfully wedded wife,
to have and to hold from this day forward,
for better, for worse,
for richer, for poorer,
in sickness and in health,
to love and to cherish,
'till death do us part.

He who finds a wife finds a good thing
and obtains favor from the Lord.
- Proverbs 18:22

Personal Reflections

1. What does Scripture reveal about God's intent for creating male and female? What roles do each gender play?

2. How can a husband model Christ's relationship with the church in marriage?

3. What are some ways in which you can become more selfless in your own life?

CHAPTER 13

Marriage is Not the End Goal

"Set your minds on things that are above,
not on things that are on earth."
- Colossians 3:2 (NASB)

All throughout my late teens and early twenties, I worked hard to prepare myself for a future spouse. I obtained a college education, got a job, paid down student loans, met the woman of my dreams, and got married. After enjoying the newness of marriage for a few months, an odd realization came over me: "Now what?" Up to that point, I had lived much of my life in anticipation of marriage. I always had a goal for myself, but now my life seemed to lack direction.

As wonderful as marriage is, it is not the final destination. Rather, marriage is meant to serve a greater objective. With this in mind, let's conclude this book by gaining a balanced view of marriage through an understanding of life's purpose.

Marriage is Not Meant to be Idolized

Being married is a wonderful gift from God, and I am thrilled to be blessed with an incredible wife. But as exhilarating as marriage is, it's important to not idolize it. As we have already learned, God requires that we "have no other gods before [Him]" (*Exodus 20:3*), and to love Him with all of our being (*Luke 10:27*). Romance, gifts, dates, and love letters are wonderful ways in which a couple can build a stronger marriage. But if a love for joy in your marriage outweighs a love for God, we worship the wrong thing.

Marriage is Not Eternal

In the Gospels, Jesus was presented with a difficult question. If a woman is widowed and remarries, who will she be married to in Heaven?

> *"Jesus replied, 'You are in error because you do not know the Scriptures or the power of God. At the resurrection people will neither marry nor be given in marriage; they will be like the angels in heaven.'" (Matthew 22:29-30, NIV)*

As wonderful as marriage is here on this earth, it does not last forever. In Heaven, we will "neither marry nor be given in marriage." Since God did not intend for marriage to be eternal, it is not the end goal. Since that is true, it must point to something greater.

Marriage is a Picture of a Greater Relationship

As studied in the last chapter, marriage is a representation of Christ's relationship with His church. Through this picture, we develop a greater appreciation of God's love for us. I can honestly say that I continue to gain a deeper understanding of how much God cares for me through my relationship with my wife. Mandy and I are learning how to love, care, and selflessly serve one another every day. These themes are a constant reminder of the daily care God shows me. In the end, marital union is an avenue which leads us to pursue a deeper relationship with our first love, Jesus.

An Eternal Focus

Do you remember the story of Chris Drager, the man who sacrificially loved his wife until the very end? Well, there is more to his story that I would like to share. His widow, Emily, kindly shared intimate details about their final days together, and the eternal focus that

Chris maintained in his perspective toward marriage. Here is what Emily wrote:

> On his deathbed, Chris emphasized that we were first and foremost brother and sister in Jesus. Since God intended for marriage to be used as a great sanctifier here on earth, there is no need for marriage in Heaven. He also reminded me that only Jesus can complete us and fill voids in our heart that no person can. Even though this might sound a little unromantic to some, this is love of the deepest and most spiritual kind.
>
> At the end, Chris's eyes were placed heavenward, and he knew he was almost home. He began to withdraw from the cares of this world—even our sweet marriage. His eyes were fixed on the Great Lover of his soul. As I began to shrink in his eyes, I felt a bit jealous, but I understood. He was going ahead. He had an accurate view of life and its cares, as we all should.
>
> Before Chris died, he gave me a ring with diamonds circling all the way around in a continuous manner. He said he liked this "eternity band" because it symbolized the sweet truth of our relationship—that while marriage is temporal, we are united together as brother and sister in Christ for all eternity. Praise God that life does not end here!

Understanding Your Purpose in Life

Since marriage is not the end goal, what is life's purpose? The answer can be found in 1 Corinthians 10:31. It says, "So, whether you eat or drink, or whatever you do, do all to the glory of God." If we are encouraged to honor God by something as trivial as eating or drinking, how much more should we give glory to God in every area of our life? As the passage says, we should do *all* for God's glory. Furthermore, Ephesians 2:10 says: "For we are his workmanship, created in Christ Jesus for good works, which God prepared beforehand, that we should walk in them."

In this passage, we learn that Christ saved us so that we might live our lives to serve His will. It's clear that life is not about self-fulfillment. Rather, let us experience the satisfaction that results from glorifying God through our service to Him in every area of our lives.

Glorify God in Marriage

Unfortunately, for some husbands, the concerns of daily life gradually wear on their motivation to invest in their marriage. But it's good to remember that loving your wife is both an act of obedience and of worship to God. You can honor God by fulfilling His command to love your wife as stated in Ephesians 5:25. You please God by showing honor and understanding to your wife as commanded in 1 Peter 3:7. God is glorified when you fulfill your wife's needs as stated in 1 Corinthians 7:3-5. Embrace marriage with the intentions of worshiping God.

Glorify God Beyond Marriage

Certainly, glorifying God does not stop with marriage. You can honor God in every area of your life. You can honor Him as a friend, a brother, or a son. You can also glorify Him as a classmate, as a church member, or as an employee. Colossians 3:23-24 says: "Whatever you do, work heartily, as for the Lord and not for men; knowing that from the Lord you will receive the inheritance as your reward. You are serving the Lord Christ." It is clear that we must serve God for His glory in everything we do.

Resolve to Live Your Life for Christ

Finally, I encourage you to learn from Paul's example. He was a single man who devoted his entire life to serving Christ. He said:

> *"For to me to live is Christ, and to die is gain. If I am to live in the flesh, that means fruitful labor for me. Yet which I shall choose I cannot tell. I am hard pressed between the two. My desire is to depart and be with Christ, for that is far better." (Philippians 1:21-23)*

For Paul, if he was alive, life was about serving Christ. If he died, life was about worshiping Christ. Paul's entire life was devoted to giving God glory. This too should be your attitude. You only have one life to live. As long as you are here on this earth, resolve to live every moment for God's glory.

"For to me to live is Christ ... "
- Philippians 1:21

Personal Reflections

1. How can a relationship become idolized? Why is marriage not the end goal in life?

2. How is loving your wife considered an act of worship to God?

3. What is your ultimate purpose in life? What changes can you make in your own life to better serve this goal?

Conclusion

"All Scripture is inspired by God and profitable for teaching,
for reproof, for correction, for training in righteousness;
so that the man of God may be adequate,
equipped for every good work."
- 2 Timothy 3:16-17 (NASB)

After reading this book, my hope is that you feel better equipped on your path to becoming the right man for the right woman. This is a vast topic with important implications. But we can take heart knowing that God provides us with all we need regarding how we should live our lives (*2 Peter 1:3*). In conclusion to this book, I thought that I would end on a few final comments to encourage you on your journey.

God Sees the Big Picture

Finding the right spouse can sometimes feel like a long journey (it certainly seemed that way for me). Because it's hard to be patient, we may feel tempted to strive ahead of God's will. In times like these, it's good to remember that He sees the bigger picture. God said in Isaiah 55:9:

> *"For as the heavens are higher than the earth, so are my ways higher than your ways and my thoughts than your thoughts."*

Since God's ways are higher than our own, we can most assuredly be at peace and trust His leading.

Use Scripture as Your Guide

Relationships can also be complicated, requiring much wisdom. Thankfully, God has given us His Word which is sufficient to guide us in all of life's circumstances. As the psalmist says, "Your word is a lamp to my feet and a light to my path" (*Psalms 119:105*). Be sure to use Scripture as a "lamp" to guide you when navigating through relationships.

Security can be Found in Obedience to God

It is good to remember that the truths revealed in God's Word are not merely a strict list of "do's" and "don'ts", or as someone said, "a list of suggestions." Rather, they are prescribed to us for our ultimate good. By obeying God and glorifying Him with our lives, naturally we reap the benefits. Psalms 18:30 says:

> *"This God—his way is perfect; the word of the Lord proves true; he is a shield for all those who take refuge in him."*

Anyone who acts in obedience to God's Word will find security. Let the Lord be your refuge in every area of life.

Diligence is Required

After reading a book such as this, it's easy to feel excited about pursuing God-honoring relationships. But it's good to be reminded that we must also be diligent in our obedience long-term. Jesus said in Luke 9:62: "No one who puts his hand to the plow and looks back is fit for the kingdom of God."

As a man who must not leave a field half-plowed, so must you be sure to endure in obedience to Christ in all areas, including your love life. Don't leave the work that God has set before you half completed.

God will Establish Your Path

As you seek to understand God's will for your life, remember that He promises to be your Guide if you trust and submit to Him. Recall Proverbs 3:5-6 which says:

> *"Trust in the Lord with all your heart and do not lean on your own understanding. In all your ways acknowledge Him, and He will make your paths straight." (Emphasis added, NASB)*

It is such a comfort to know that we can entrust our future and well-being into the hands of our loving God. You can be sure that God will take care of you when you lean on Him. "The Lord makes firm the steps of the one who delights in him" (*Psalms 37:23, NIV*).

Becoming the Right Man before God

Hopefully, after reading this book, it's clear that "becoming Mr. Right" involves a lot more than just learning how to be a good boyfriend. Rather, it has much more to do with becoming the right man before God. When you prioritize honoring God in your own life, you can trust that God will lead you to the right woman.

As you continue in your journey to "Becoming Mr. Right," I want to leave you with a final encouragement to position your focus to glorifying God. When your eyes are on Him, His hand will be on you. Make Paul's words your prayer:

> *" ... forgetting what lies behind and reaching forward to what lies ahead, I press on toward the goal for the prize of the upward call of God in Christ Jesus."*
> *- Philippians 3:13-14, NASB*

Appendices

APPENDIX A

Preparing to Provide

Developing a Strong Work Ethic

In order to become a sufficient provider, you will need to maintain a job. Once you are in a work environment, much will be expected of you. This means that you must cast aside laziness, and establish a good work ethic. Proverbs 6:6-11 says:

> *"Go to the ant, O sluggard; consider her ways, and be wise. Without having any chief, officer, or ruler, she prepares her bread in summer and gathers her food in harvest. How long will you lie there, O sluggard? When will you arise from your sleep? A little sleep, a little slumber, a little folding of the hands to rest, and poverty will come upon you like a robber, and want like an armed man."*

How would you characterize your life? Is most of your time consumed with entertainment? Do you waste countless hours on movies and games? Or do you keep busy with education, hard work, and helping others? In order to provide for a future family, you must be willing to work hard. Let the diligent ant be your example, and begin developing a good work ethic in your life.

Selecting a Career

You may be wondering, "How do I discover which career path is right for me?" The first thing you should do is pray for God to give you wisdom on this matter. 1 John 5:15 says: ":And if we know that he hears us in whatever we ask, we know that we have the requests that we have asked of him. When you make a pure-hearted request to God, He will give you the wisdom you need in pursuing a career. Then, it is good to account for the gifts that God has given you. 1 Peter 4:10 says: "As each has received a gift, use it to serve one another, as good stewards of God's varied grace."

God gives everyone natural gifts that can be used to His glory. Although it's not mandatory, shaping your career around your gifts may enable you to be more effective and enjoy your work. For instance, if you possess natural leadership qualities, perhaps you should consider going into management. If you love interaction and helping others, maybe consider pursuing a career which involves being a good communicator. If you are the "problem-solving" type, a technical field may be a good fit for you.

Next, I would urge you to be thoughtful in your career choice. Luke 14:28-30 says:

> *"For which of you, desiring to build a tower, does not first sit down and count the cost, whether he has enough to complete it? Otherwise, when he has laid a foundation and is not able to finish, all who see it begin to mock him, saying, 'This man began to build and was not able to finish.'"*

Even though Jesus was using this illustration to urge people to consider the cost of discipleship, some practical wisdom can be gleaned from this example. It's important to be a thoughtful and careful planner, especially when choosing a career path. Otherwise, you could spend a lot of time and money preparing for an education that you never use in the end.

Also, do yourself a favor by researching the average wages associated with specific majors and trades. Pursue a career that will be meaningful, but also enable you to successfully provide for your future family.

Learning How to Control Finances

As a future provider, it will be important for you to know how to handle finances. Proverbs 3:9-10 says, "Honor the Lord with your wealth and with the first fruits of all your produce; then your barns will be filled with plenty, and your vats will be bursting with wine." God requires you to honor Him with your "wealth," and your wealth will determine your family's quality of life. So it is vital to start learning how to handle finances.

A great way to start practicing financial responsibility is to establish a budget. A budget is a way to control and estimate how much money you have and spend in a given period of time. For instance, if you want to limit yourself to spend roughly $50/month on restaurants, then you allot $50 of your paycheck to be specifically reserved for that. You must also make sure that you do *not* spend over that amount. Simply put, it's a great way to know where your money is going as opposed to spending without limits.

If you want to learn more about the basics of finance, feel free to visit my website at www.lifespringministries.net. There you will find references to some great financial resources which will teach you the basics of budgeting, saving, investing, and more.

APPENDIX B

Singleness

Many people wonder if God has destined them to lifelong singleness. Some dread the thought of living life alone. As a result, many set out on a desperate search to find anyone that might take them. But, if it's God's will for you to marry, waiting for the right person at the right time is worth it. And, if you're meant to be single, embracing God's will for your life will bring true happiness. Let's now take a brief look at what the Bible has to say about singleness.

Being Single is a Good Thing

While Scripture clearly reveals that being married is good (*Proverbs. 18:22*), it also describes singleness as being good. Paul says:

> *"I want you to be free from anxieties. The unmarried man is anxious about the things of the Lord, how to please the Lord. But the married man is anxious about worldly things, how to please his wife, and his interests are divided ... I say this for your own benefit, not to lay any restraint upon you, but to promote good order and to secure your undivided devotion to the Lord." (1 Corinthians 7:32-35)*

As you can see, Paul makes it clear that those who are single have an advantage. They can effectively serve the Lord without distraction. If God has not yet revealed your future soulmate to you, then take advantage of the time to serve the Lord. Singles are just as complete in Christ as those who are married.

Should I Stay single?

Do you find yourself asking, "Should I stay single?" The Apostle Paul has valuable insight on this topic. He himself was a single man who devoted his life to serving Christ. He says:

> *"I wish that all were as I myself am. But each has his own gift from God, one of one kind and one of another. To the unmarried and the widows I say that it is good for them to remain single as I am. But if they cannot exercise self-control, they should marry. For it is better to marry than to burn with passion" (1 Corinthians 7:7-9).*

Remaining single is not a command. But Paul does provide encouragement to those who have the ability to control their longings for marital intimacy to remain single. If you find yourself fitting this description and don't "burn with passion," perhaps you should prayerfully consider if singleness is God's will for your life.

Contentment in Waiting

If you have a strong desire to marry but are still single, the wait can sometimes be difficult. If you struggle in this area, I would encourage you to dwell on the "Contentment" chapter of this book. This section will encourage you to find the "secret" to contentment through trusting the Lord, delighting in Him, serving and praying. As you seek God, you can rest assured that He loves you, and has your best in mind.

> *" ... for I have learned to be content in whatever circumstances I am. I know how to get along with humble means, and I also know how to live in prosperity; in any and every circumstance I have learned the secret of being filled and going hungry,*

both of having abundance and suffering need. I can do all things through Him who strengthens me." (Philippians 4:11-13)

APPENDIX C

Breaking Up

Perhaps, after reading this book, you've realized that you're in an unhealthy relationship. Maybe you're wondering if you need to break up with the girl you are dating. This is a delicate subject to address and there is no perfect formula on how to break up, but I hope to provide a little guidance on how you can approach this area.

Is a Breakup Necessary?

A good question to ask yourself is, "Is a breakup really necessary?" Some cases may be clear. Perhaps the girl you're interested in is not saved, and has no desire to respond to the Gospel. Maybe she's consistently proven that she is not teachable, and isn't willing to change certain sin patterns in her life. Maybe you've realized that you're not ready practically or spiritually, and need time to grow. Or perhaps you're in a relationship for all the wrong reasons.

In other cases, the decision may not be as clear or necessary. Perhaps you are bothered by sin issues in her life, but haven't brought them to her attention yet. Maybe she just needed someone to help her see a blind spot, and she's willing to change. Maybe certain sins exist in either yours or her life, but there is evidence of growth.

To determine if a breakup is needed, you will need wisdom. This will require much prayer (*Philippians 4:6*) and counsel (*Proverbs 15:22*). Ultimately, you are going to need God's help to make the right decision. Consider the following admonitions:

Be Clear

If God does lead you to decide that a breakup is necessary, then often a conversation will have to take place. There are special cases where communication should be cut off immediately (perhaps in cases of temptation, safety, etc.), but under normal circumstances you should speak to the girl in person if possible. She should not receive an e-mail, text, etc., saying "Hey, we're done." A breakup should also not be so ambiguous that a girl is left wondering, "Why is he not talking to me anymore?" It's important to be clear, and not create confusion which can cause the relationship to be drawn out longer than it needs to be.

When breaking up with the girl, you must come prayerfully prepared. You will need to know why you are breaking up, and be ready to give an answer to her questions. You will need to be clear, and speak words that are only "fitting" for the moment. Proverbs 25:11 says, "A word fitly spoken is like apples of gold in a setting of silver."

Be Kind

When breaking up, your words should also be kind and loving. 1 Corinthians 13:2 says:

> *" ... and if I have prophetic powers, and understand all mysteries and all knowledge, and if I have all faith, so as to remove mountains, but have not love, I am nothing." The fact is that if you speak without compassion, all your efforts are meaningless.*

Your words should also not be filled with bitterness, accusations, or anger. Proverbs 15:1 says: "A soft answer turns away wrath, but a harsh word stirs up anger."

In addition, you must also be cautious about what to say and what not to say. Proverbs 10:19 says: "When words are many, transgression